150

PSALMS
FOR
TEENS

ELDON WEISHEIT

CPH
SAINT LOUIS

Cover design by Karol Bergdolt.

Scripture quotations are taken from the HOLY BIBLE NEW
INTERNATIONAL VERSION®. NIV®. Copyright© 1973, 1978,
1984 by International Bible Society. Used by permission of
Zondervan Publishing House. All rights reserved.

Note on Psalm 35: Excerpted from Mark R. Etter
and Diane J. Grebing, *Life Light: Selected Psalms,*
©1997 Concordia Publishing House. Used by permission.

Copyright© 1992, 1994, 2002 by Concordia Publishing House
3558 S. Jefferson Ave., St. Louis MO 63118-3968

Manufactured in the United States of America.

1 2 3 4 5 6 7 8 9 10   11 10 09 08 07 06 05 04 03 02

INTRO DUCTION

Teen, these psalms are for you. But there's something I want to explain: The psalms in this book are not the psalms of the Bible. But I did study them—a lot—to see what their authors (often King David) were feeling when they wrote. I tried to feel what they felt, both in the situation in their lives and in their relationship with God. Then, as I wrote this book, I kept one eye on the biblical psalms and one eye on you.

The psalms are different from other books of the Bible. Much of the Bible is history, the stories you heard in Sunday school. The stories that show that God is a part of human history. He made the world and stuck with it. He is part of the conversations in the Bible. He is one of the actors—that is, one who causes the action to happen. In fact, God was so eager to have a leading role in world history that He applied for citizenship and became a human being named Jesus Christ. The stories about

Jesus show us what God says and does when He lives with us.

Part of the Bible gives us theology—that is, knowledge of God. The Old Testament prophets spoke and wrote the message of God for the people. The New Testament evangelists wrote letters that explain how God's action applies to the everyday lives of people. The theology of the Bible is not a vague feeling or a human philosophy; it says that God is real and we can depend on Him. Scripture recognizes all the problems and joys, strengths and weakness of people and tells us that God knows what is going on and that He is here to help.

Although the psalms contain both history and theology, they look at a situation from a different point of view. Psalms, by definition, are sacred songs and poems for the praise of God: worship. When God's people know His track record (history) and the way He thinks (theology),

they want to rejoice with Him (worship). The biblical psalms are great worship aids because they show us that those who wrote them had learned their lessons about God.

The psalms reveal also the feelings of their authors. The Psalter (the book of Psalms) contains a catalog of human feelings—expressions of joy and sadness, trust and doubt, fear and faith, despair and hope, loneliness and security. At times, some of the psalm writers seem to be paranoid. At other times, they show faith that is on a solid rock.

These people were not afraid to reveal their emotions because they knew God. When they were happy, they praised God. When they were scared, they blamed God. When they were angry at God, they told Him so. Some readers have been shocked to see that, at times, a writer of a psalm may have doubted God's presence or even asked Him to do wrong things. But that's the point. When the psalmist had feelings that caused them problems, they told God—and He helped them. The psalms are God's success stories. They are written by the people who heard Him and knew they could talk to Him about anything.

As I said, I wrote my psalms in this book with one eye on the Bible and the other on you. If the psalm writer talked about his king and nation, I thought about your government leaders and country. If he talked about going to temple, I thought about your place in church. If he told God what made him happy or sad, angry or afraid, I thought about the things that might cause you to feel the same way.

As I wrote, I did not try to pretend that I was a teenager. I was a parish pastor and worked with many people of all ages. However I especially enjoyed confirmation classes. I think that I can recognize and identify with your life experiences just as I can with the people who wrote the biblical psalms.

My purpose in this book is to bring their and your experiences together. I hope this process will help you express your feelings (all of them) to God. Think about what you have learned about God (history and theology), and use those things in your worship life. Your application may be very different from mine; that's fine. You might even like to write your own psalms. I hope that as you read my psalms, you will go back and read the ones in the Bible. After all, it's God's Word that prompts us to worship Him. I pray that my words will encourage you to do exactly the same.

Eldon Weisheit

PSALM 1

PSALM 2

You will have more fun if you don't listen to those who tell you to do wrong things,

if you don't follow those who lead you to dangerous places,

if you don't go along with those who do not love God.

You will be better off if you listen to God,

hear the stories about Jesus,

and praise God in your heart.

Then you will be like a tree that grows tall and straight.

You will be able to do many things well.

But those who don't know God, who do not hear His Word and learn how to do what is right,

they are like weeds that make a mess and must be pulled up and thrown away.

God wants to lead you because He knows where it is best for you to go.

Why do parents yell at me?

Why do teachers assign things that I can't do?

Bullies laugh at me and call me bad names.

They say that I'm stupid because I go to church.

They even say bad things about Jesus.

But Jesus is with me.

He laughs with me, not at me.

He tells me that others can't hurt me because He loves me and is with me.

"I will tell those people that you are My friend," Jesus says.

I am glad that He takes care of me.

PSALM 4

PSALM 3

Please listen to me, God.

A long time ago, when I was a little kid, when I was lost in the shopping center, I prayed—
and You heard me.
Be kind to me now and hear my prayer.

A lot of people are mad at me.
They talk about me behind my back.
To my face they say that You won't help me.

But that's not true, is it, God?
You have helped me before.
I know it.
I'm scared now.
But I've been scared before, and You helped me.
So I'm asking You to help again.
I know You will.

How long will people make fun of me?
How long will I feel ugly?
How long will I feel stupid?

I know You picked me to be Your friend.
I know You love me and help me.
But I want them to like me, too.
Help me like them so they can like me.

I'm ready to go to sleep now.
I'm not going to worry anymore because I asked You to help.

Then, when I go to sleep, I can feel good.
God, You're the only one who can help me.

Come on, God!
You can do it!

PSALM 5

Please listen to me, God.
I have to talk to You.
I need someone to help,
and You're the only one who can.

It's time for me to get out of bed.
I want You to be with me today.
I've got to know that You know
I'm here.

You aren't happy when I do bad
things.
I know that.
You don't like lies and angry
words.
I know that.

But I also know that You love me.
You want me to talk to You.
You want us to be together.

And that's my problem, God.
Some of my friends don't know
You.
And some don't like you.
When I am with them,
I may forget You, too.

So please hear me now, God.
Love me so much that I will
remember You all day.

PSALM 6

God, don't be mad at me!
Please don't punish me.
I know I do bad things.
But I still need You to be on my side.
I'm waiting for You to help me.

I cried last night before I went to sleep.
I wanted to cry at school today, but I drew pictures in my book instead, and I pushed the other kids in the lunch line.

Can You hear my crying,
God, even when I'm not crying?
Please help me now!

PSALM 7

God, I need You!

Please hide me!

Protect me from those who find fault with me.

They want to make me feel bad about myself.

They want me to think that I am no good.

God, if I have done wrong,

I need Your help.

Was I wrong when I told my parents what I thought,
even though I knew they wouldn't like it?

Am I bad because I think about sex?

Am I no good because sometimes I don't want to go to church?

You have to help me, Lord!

Those at school who don't know You say I'm bad
because I don't do what they want.

Those at church who say they know everything about You say I'm bad because I don't do what they want.

How do I know, Lord?

You are the only judge that counts, Lord.

You are the only one who can judge with innocent eyes and a holy heart.

You judge by what You see in my heart, not by what
others say, and not even by what I say.

I don't always know what is right and what is wrong.

I know many who want to tell me, but I need someone who shows me.

And that's You, Jesus—only You.

You're the only one who forgives me when I am wrong.

Therefore I'll let You judge me.

God, You are my bodyguard.

You're the one who makes me feel safe, even when I am in dangerous company.

People do lots of bad things all the time.

You already know that, Lord; so it's not that I am telling on them.

But I don't have to be afraid because there is evil in the world because You're here, too.

I was taught that original sin meant that sin came as standard equipment on us all.

But I think some people try to find new ways to sin.

They want to claim originality for their evil.

But You know them, Lord, just as You know me.

I'm not afraid of their evil because You will take care of it.

I like Your justice, God, because it comes wrapped in mercy.

PSALM 9

PSALM 8

God, You are the best!
You are so great that You don't need famous people to say how great You are.
Even a little baby can do it.

I like to look at all the beautiful things that You have made: The moon and the stars, the trees and the flowers, the birds and the bugs.

The other things You made don't give You any trouble.
But I do. (And other people do too.)
Why do You still like us people, God?
You have given us so much.
And we can do so many fun things.

I like the way You run this world, God!

I want to tell everyone what You have done, God.
You make me so happy that I want to tell everyone.

The bullies are afraid to pick on me because You are my friend.
You are always fair, and You keep them from hurting me.

You're good to other people, too.
Sometimes I want to be the bully, but You won't let me.

You love the new kid in class who acts like a nerd to get attention.
You care about the one who can't play ball and made our team lose.
You never forget anyone.

Thanks for taking good care of us.
And, oh yes:
Please take good care of Yourself, too; because without You, we're in big trouble.

PSALM 10

Why do You hide from me, God?
Why is it that when I need You
the most,
You seem the least available?

Do You know what people get
away with around here?
Can't You see what is going on?
I've no complaints about how You
take care of me.
I appreciate my home, country,
school, food, health, and all that
stuff.
Thank You for those gifts—and I
mean it!

But how about those other peo-
ple?
You take care of them just as well
as You take care of me.
And look what they do, Lord.
Look!

I don't mean just the ones who
smoke; or the ones who drink
beer in the parking lot.
I don't mean just those who steal;
or the ones who look at Internet
porn.
I don't mean just those who have
sex with anyone and then have
abortions.
I mean everyone, God!

Even the good ones are proud.
They want people to see their
clothes and grades.
They want to tell about their trips
and cars.
They laugh at poor people.
They hate people who are differ-
ent.

It scares me, Lord, because I don't
see anyone who is good.
But I do see You, Lord.
I know You love us all.
Please help me help others, but
help me never hurt others.
Please help others help me, but
help them never hurt me.

We all need Your help, Lord.

PSALM 11

I know that God knows—He knows what I say and what I do.

He knows what I think and what I feel. Yet He loves me.

I feel safe with Him.

Don't tell me, "Come on, no one will know."

No one can hide from God.

God doesn't live in a church building or up on a mountain.

His temple is everything He created.

He doesn't just wave to us or leave us messages on paper.

He was born as a baby named Jesus, who had a family, a church, a school—like we do.

God is with us.

Whether we do good or bad, it makes no difference; He is here.

Some people are afraid of God.

They think He will find out about them.

But I am not afraid because I know He already knows.

PSALM 12

Please help me, God!

I can't trust anyone but You.

All the kids are bad.

They cheat at school.

They lie all the time.

They pretend they like each other, but they don't.

Make them shut up, God.

Don't let them say, "I'll do what I want!"

"I'll say what I want!"

"You can't stop me!"

And God said to me: "I will be with you, because you need Me.

I will be with them, because they need Me.

I will help you and them, because you all need Me."

I will always have to live with bad people.

Help me, God, so I won't follow them and do the bad things they do.

PSALM 13

Hey, God, how long are You going to forget me?
Forever?
How much longer will You hide up there by Yourself?
How much longer do I have to hurt like this?
How much longer will I want to cry all day long—and all night too?

Look at me, God!
Talk to me—now!

Don't let me be alone with people who hurt me.
I'm counting on You to help me, God.
I know You'll help me again.

The dumb kids say, "There is no God."
They are the ones who say bad things and do bad things.

But I know there is a God and He watches us.
He is looking for kids to say good things and to do good things.

Even though we all do wrong things—me too—God watches over us all.
And God asks: "Don't they know who I am?
Don't they know that I know what they do?"

I guess they're scared of You, God.
That's why they say You aren't real.

But I know You will help us 'cause Jesus is on our side.
We will be glad when we all know You.

PSALM 16

PSALM 15

God: Who can be Your friend?
Who can sit on Your lap?

I know who: The ones who know
You help them do good things.
The ones who like to hear what
You say.
The ones who like the people that
You like.

God, You are my friend.
I am glad.

Take good care of me, God, so I
won't get hurt.
I tell You, "You are my God."
Thanks for the good things that
You have given me.

Kids who don't know You don't
know about all the good things
You do.
I will tell them that You lead me
where I should go, that You are
always with me, that nothing can
scare me.

You show me the way that leads
to life.
Being with You makes me happy!

I love You so much, God!
You watch over me.
You take care of me.
You hug me when I hurt.
When I have troubles, I ask You
for help, and You help me.

Please LISTEN, God! I want You
to be fair.
I want to tell You how I feel.

I know You are on my side.
You know me.
You have looked at me.
You have watched me.
And You still love me.

Sometimes I think about dying.
My mom, my dad—or I—might
die.
Then I remember You, God, and
they do too.
Even if they or I die, we will be
with You.

I pray to You, God, because You
listen to me and answer my
prayers.
I know Your Son, and He said I
could use His name as a reference
when I talk to You.

Sometimes I think about car
wrecks, robbers, or a fire that
could burn our home.
We might have an earthquake or a
war.

I'm scared of some people.
I'm afraid when I think about
some things.
But when I wake up every morn-
ing, I know You are with me.
That makes me happy.

Sometimes I worry that my parents might get a divorce or they
might lose their jobs and we
would be poor.

I worry about a lot of things, God.
But I also remember You.
You have always helped me
before.
You will always help me, won't
You?

God, when I look at the sky, I can tell what You have been doing.

The sun, the moon, and the stars show that You keep things going all the time.

Every morning the sun shows us that You are still on the job.

Each night is Your promise for another day.

I don't need to hear Your voice.

I can hear what You are saying when I see what You do.

PSALM 19

Everything You say, God, is right.

You know what I should do and what I should not do.

You are fair in everything You do.

Whatever You decide is always right.

You're so smart that we can't even give You a grade.

I like Your rules, but I can't follow all of them.

I've probably done some wrong things that I don't even know about.

Just in case, forgive me for those things, too.

Please listen to the things I think.

You are the one who understands me.

PSALM 20

If you've got a problem, tell God about it.

He has helped me; He'll help you, too.

You can hear about Him at church.

He'll listen to your prayers.

He'll give you what is good for you.

Some kids think their parents will always take care of them.

Some think they can take care of themselves.

But I think we should let God take care of us.

You will hear us and help us, won't You, God?

PSALM 21

I watched the president today, Lord. He's always on TV. Everyone knows him.

People always take his picture.

What he says is important.

Look what You have given to him, God.

He has a fancy house and bodyguards.

He must be very rich.

He never has to mow his yard or take out the garbage like my dad does.

He will be in history books for my kids to read about.

But the president needs You, too.

He needs someone to talk to and who won't tell reporters what he said.

He needs someone to thank when things go great or when nothing goes wrong.

He needs to know that Jesus is his Savior, just as I do.

Thanks, God, for helping me.

Please help our president, too.

PSALM 22— ECHOES

"My God, my God, why have You forsaken me?" (Psalm 22:1)

"Jesus cried out in a loud voice,... 'My God, My God, why have You forsaken Me?'" (Matthew 27:46)

All who see me make fun of me, they stick out their tongues and shake their heads.

"You relied on the Lord," they say.

"Why doesn't He save you?"

"All who see me mock me; they hurl insults, shaking their heads: 'He trusts in the Lord; let the Lord rescue him. Let Him deliver him, since he delights in Him.'" (Psalm 22:7–8)

"Then they spit in His face and struck Him with their fists. Others slapped Him and said, 'Prophesy to us, Christ. Who hit You?'" (Matthew 26:67) "They spit on Him, and took the staff and struck Him on the head again and again." (Matthew 27:30) "[They] mocked Him 'He saved others,' they said, 'but He can't save Himself!'" (Matthew 27:41–42)

"My strength is dried up like a potsherd, and my tongue sticks to the roof of my mouth." (Psalm 22:15)

"Jesus said, 'I am thirsty.'" (John 19:28)

"They divide my garments among them and cast lots for my clothing." (Psalm 22:18)

"When the soldiers crucified Jesus, they took His clothes, dividing them into four shares... 'Let's not tear it,' they said to one another. 'Let's decide by lot who will get it.'" (John 19:23–24)

"All the rich of the earth will feast and worship; all who go down to the dust will kneel before Him—those who cannot keep themselves alive." (Psalm 22:29)

"That at the name of Jesus every knee should bow, in heaven and on earth and under the earth, and every tongue confess that Jesus Christ is Lord, to the glory of God the Father." (Philippians 2:10–11)

PSALM 23

When David was a boy, he took care of sheep—and perhaps dreamed of being the king some day. When he became the king of Israel, he dreamed about the times when he was a boy taking care of the sheep.

David knew God had been good to him. He wanted to tell the people of Israel how God took care of them. So he talked to the people about God as a shepherd:

The Lord is my shepherd; I have everything I need.

He lets me rest in fields of green grass and leads me to quiet pools of fresh water.

He gives me new strength.

He guides me in the right paths, as He has promised.

Then an unusual thing happened. As David talked to the people about God, his mind wandered. He forgot that he was talking to the people, and he started talking to God:

Even if I go through the deepest darkness, I will not be afraid, Lord, for You are with me.

Your shepherd's rod and staff protect me.

You prepare a banquet for me where all my enemies can see me; You welcome me as an honored guest and fill my cup to the brim.

I know that Your goodness and love will be with me all my life, and Your house will be my home as long as I live.

When David talked to God, he remembered how loving and kind God is. So he talked to the people about God.

When David talked to the people about God, he also remembered how loving and kind God is. So he talked to God.

Lord, when I talk to You, help me to remember others.

Lord, when I talk to others, help me to remember You.

PSALM 24

God, You've got it all!
You made the earth and the space it spins in.
You drew the plans.
You made the building blocks.
You put it all together.
It's all Yours!

Who can get an appointment to see You?
Who can drop by Your house for a visit?
Who can get Your unlisted number?
Only someone who is perfect can get through to You.

But listen, God!
Pay attention!
You've got an appointment in Your book.
There's a knock at Your door.
Your phone is ringing.
Sit down in Your chair.
Open the door. Answer the phone.
You've got company!

Who is this that can get through to You?
Who is this who is welcomed by You?

It is Jesus!
It is the one who came from You to us so He could die for our sins.

Now He comes from us to You.
Now Jesus makes an appointment with You.
He knocks on Your door.
He rings Your bell.
And He brings us along!

Get ready, God!
You're going to have lots of company!

PSALM 25

I've got to talk to You, God…
'cause I can't trust anyone else.

They call me a loser.
They laugh at me and point their
fingers at me.
How can I be a loser when I trust in
You?
How can they be winners when
they say bad things about You?

Will You help me understand, Lord?
I can see how You run things, but I
want to know why.
Why do You do things the way You
do them?

I'm going to trust You even though
it doesn't make sense to me sometimes.

Remember what kind of a God You
are, Lord.
You are the one who got the idea to
send Jesus to be a human with us.
You are the one who offered Him as
the one to die to pay for our sins.

After You remember those things,
then remember me.
When You remember what I've
done wrong, remember Jesus died
for me.
When You see the mistakes I make,
see the Savior I have.

Then teach me, Lord.
I've learned what I should do and
what I should not do.
Now would You teach me how to
do what I should do and not to do
what I should not do?
Learning the Ten Commandments
hasn't been enough for me.
I still need Your help.
So let's start again, Friend.

I've asked You for help, Lord, over
and over again.
And I know You've helped me.
Here I am again.

Please listen with a kind ear 'cause
I'm in the pits.
I'm scared.
I'm lonely.
I'm confused.
I've dug my way into lots of prob-
lems again.
Will You pull me out again?

Look at all the problems I have.
Look at all the things that could
hurt me.
Please protect me.
I've got to trust You because I don't
know anyone else who understands.

I know You've got a lot of other
people, too, who depend on You.
Please help them also.

PSALM 26

Jesus, I want You to judge my case.

You are the only one who will find me "not guilty."

Look at me, Lord.

Listen to what I say.

Read my mind, not my lips.

Read my heart, not my actions.

You have let me in on Your secret.

When others judge me, when I judge myself, I am guilty.

But with You I am a different person.

You see me through the gift that You gave me.

In Your eyes, I am forgiven

When You search me, You find Your grace, the gift You gave me.

That's why I like to worship You.

I want to hear Your Word; I want to receive You in the Supper You gave us.

I like to talk to You and listen to You.

When You are with me, I can be what You want me to be.

PSALM 27

Lord, You're the one who knows the way to go.
I'm not scared when You're the only one around.
But sometimes I am scared when I am with others.
Some kids offer me drugs at school.
They say I won't even have to pay.
They'll give them to me—the first time.
And I'm scared.

I thought Chris was one of my friends.
But yesterday Chris showed me a magazine with dirty pictures.
Chris wants me to do something that I don't want to do.
And I'm scared.

I ask You, Lord, for one thing—that is, one thing for today:
Please keep me close to You.
I want You to be with me.
I want You to guide me.
I want You to protect me.

Why should I do what others want me to do?
Do they really want to help me?
If I follow them, I will be like others who do those things.
And I don't like that.

I'd rather do what You want me to do.
You care about me.
You will help me be the kind of person You made me to be.

Lord, listen to me when I talk to You.
I need an answer from You, and I need it now.

You invited me.
You said, "Come, worship Me."
I answered, "I will come, Lord."
So don't back out now.

Don't be mad at me, even though You have good reasons.
My parents are angry at me. They feel like giving up on me.
But, please Lord, don't You give up.

Let me know what You want me to do, Lord. Make it real clear.
I admit I haven't done what You have told me to do, and I've done things You told me not to do.
But don't give up on me.

I know I can do better with Your help.
I trust You
And I trust You to trust me.

PSALM 28

God, be my big brother!
Be six feet tall.
Look like You're on the football
team.
Don't shave for three days.
Then walk with me down the hall
so no one will knock my books
out of my hands.
Sit with me in the cafeteria so oth-
ers will want to be at my table.
Stand beside me when I have to
give my presentation to the class.

Make them sorry that they have
hurt me.
Show them the ways You have
helped me.
Let them see what it's like to have
You as a friend.

I want to praise You, Lord.
I want to let others know how
great You are.
But You've got to do Your part.
I know how great You are.
You've got to learn to show off a
little.

Shall we do it my way or Yours?

PSALM 29

God, You are the greatest!
You've got it all!
You've done it all!
You are the greatest (to put it
mildly)!

I can hear You speak among the
roar at the game.
I can hear Your Word over the
sounds of the band.

Your voice tells me You are with
me.
I hear Your love by seeing what
You do.
This world that You made is a
great place to live.
God, You're the greatest!

PSALM 30

Thank You, God, for saving me—for saving me from me.

I thought everyone was laughing at me. Everything I did was wrong. I even wanted to laugh at myself, but it wasn't funny.

I wanted You to help, Lord.
I asked You to let me die.
But since You wouldn't do it, I thought about how I might do it myself.

Then I asked You to help again.

Thank You, God, for saying yes to my second prayer and not the first.

I will remember what You have done. My fear and anger were for only a night. Your love and patience are forever.

I may be scared at night, but You are there in the morning.

Now I feel safe and secure.

I used to feel worthless, and I wanted to die.

But I asked You: "What do I gain by dying? Can dead people enjoy life more than unhappy living people?"

Dying like that is a waste, a stupid waste.

You have changed my desire to die into a desire to live.

You are my God, the only one I've got.

I will thank You forever.

PSALM 31

I need Your help, God.
Don't let me get hurt.
Hear me!
Save me now!
Be my bodyguard.
Don't let anyone hurt me.

They have set a trap for me.
They are using friendship as bait.
If I want to be one of the crowd, if
I want to sit at their table, if I
want to ride in their car, I have to
take the bait.

But it's a trap.
A trap that will make me say
things I don't want to say and do
things I don't want to do.
God, You can see what I want, and
You can see what I will have to do
to get it.
Help me, God; I'm in trouble.
I don't have to hide my tears from
You.
I'm tired of crying.
I'm tired of feeling that I am
alone.
They are all making fun of me.
Some of them point their fingers
at me and call me names.
Worse yet, others don't even
notice that I am here.

Will You help me, God?
Love me, and love me again even
more.
Don't let me make a fool of
myself.
Don't let me believe their lies.
Help me see what will happen if I
walk into their trap.

Thank You, God, for listening.
You have helped me.
Now would You help them... and
keep them off my back?

PSALM 32

What a relief!
I feel so clean, so new.
You have forgiven me, Lord!
You have taken me back into Your arms.
I can look at You again and smile.
Thank You, God.

When I refused to admit that I was wrong, I was miserable all the time.
I couldn't talk to You (except when I prayed before eating).
I felt dirty.
I was sad even when I laughed.

Then I said it.
I told You what You already knew.
I admitted what I had done.
The words I had to use were embarrassing, but I said them to You.
And You forgave me!

I was drowning in my sin until I climbed to the cross.
Others may understand my sins because they are guilty, too.
But You can forgive because You are not guilty, yet You died for me.
Thank You, Lord.

God says:
I will teach you.
Will you learn?
I know what is after tomorrow and what is around the corner.
Will you learn from Me?

Don't be stupid like a horse or a mule that must be guided by bridle and a bit in its mouth.

Learn to think, to make decisions, to be responsible for yourself.

I will teach you. I love you and want you to be with Me.

PSALM 33

Let's hear it for God!
Look at what He has done for us.
Let the music play!
Let's dance and sing!
We've got something to be happy
about.

God is our friend.
He makes promises and keeps
them.
He loves us so much that He
wants to be with us.

The Lord made the earth, the faraway star, and the close-up atom.
Everything we touch, see, hear,
smell, and taste has been made
by Him.
Praise the Lord!

The Lord looks down from heaven
to watch over us and protect us.
He sent Jesus to be here with us
and to save us from ourselves.
He knows everything we do and
everything we think.
And He still loves us.
Praise the Lord!

We don't have to depend on big
armies or big bank accounts.

The Lord takes care of us.
We can trust in Him.
Praise the Lord!

PSALM 34

Come, my young friends, and listen to me, and I will teach you to honor the Lord.

Learn to thank the Lord.

See and understand what He has done.

Join with others in praising Him.

Come, my young friends, and listen to me, and I will teach you to honor the Lord.

Learn to pray to the Lord when you need His help.

He helps those who know they are helpless.

He sends His angels to those in danger.

Come, my young friends, and listen to me, and I will teach you to honor the Lord.
Learn for yourself how good God is.
Rely on Him to take care of you.
Even the strong and the rich don't have everything they want.
Trust God to provide for you.

Come, my young friends, and listen to me, and I will teach you to honor the Lord.
Learn how to enjoy life and how to be happy.
Don't do the things that hurt you and others.
Do the things and say the words that give peace and joy.

Come, my young friends, and listen to me, and I will teach you to honor the Lord.
Learn to listen to what God has to say.
He wants to help you; He's on your side.
Life may be confusing, but He's your guide.

Come, my young friends, and listen to me, and I will teach you to honor the Lord.
Learn that all suffering is not punishment from God.
It's your way to grow, to understand others.
Christ has suffered, too, so you need never hurt alone.

Come, my young friends, and listen to me, and I will teach you to honor the Lord.

PSALM 35

I want my enemies to be Your enemies, Lord.

They have no reason not to like me.

They just think it's fun to pick on me.

They want to make themselves look good by making me look bad.

But I am not bad.

I may be different.

I may not be like them or talk like them, but I am not bad.

I know You have created me, God.

And, Jesus, You are on my side.

I am not bad.

When I try to be nice to them, they ignore me.

When I do something good for them, they hurt me.

When they couldn't do their homework, I helped them.

I treated them like friends.

But when I got in trouble, they laughed at me.

They lied about me so other people wouldn't like me.

Isn't it time for You to help me,
Lord?
I will give You credit.
I will thank You and tell others
what You have done.

They are not my friends.
They tell bad things about me and
point their fingers at me and say,
"We saw what you did."
It's Your turn Lord.
Wake up and show them who You
are.

Lord, I just noticed something.
There are others who do like me.
They need friends, just as I do.
They would be glad to talk to me,
to come to my house, to eat with
me, to walk with me between
classes.

Help me, Lord.
Help me see those who do like
me, so I don't spend all my time
thinking about those who hurt
me.

* Psalm 35 is one of a group (Psalms 35,
58, 69, 137) called Imprecatory Psalms.
These psalms are the cries of a people in
pain appealing to God for help. While the
language may seem harsh, the psalmists
consider their enemies to be the enemies of
God who must be judged so God's name
and reputation are cleared. These psalms
are not psalms of personal vendetta, but
psalms reflecting God's calling to lead the
fight against evil.

PSALM 36

I can't see You today, God, because my sin has come between You and me.

My sin tells me that You can't hear me.

It says that You're not even there; and if You were there, You wouldn't care about me.

My sin tells me that if I want to get what I want, I should forget You and go for it.

I like me better when I'm with You than when I'm with my sin.

So that's why I'm talking to You.

I told my sin I was going to tell on it.

And I'm telling You.

Jesus, I can see that Your love starts with me, but I can't see where it ends.

You love is higher than the trees, the mountains, the moon, the farthest star.

Is there no limit to Your love?

I can think about things that are close by and of everyday events— my teddy bear that I still keep (just in case), my family, my special place in the backyard, and other good things in life.

And I can think about things far away and beyond what I will ever see—an island in the south Pacific, a crater on the moon, a black hole in faraway space.

But Your love is both here and there, with the teddy bear and the black hole.

Thank You, Jesus, for being a part of my little world.

Thank You, Jesus, for letting me be a part of Your world beyond all worlds.

PSALM 37

"When you have to make a choice," they told me, "make two lists so you can see what each choice offers."

Here are my two lists:

What Sin Offers

1. A lot of attention and everybody knows my name.

2. I can take from others, and I can get even.

3. Power to hurt those who are not as strong or as smart as I.

4. When good happens, I get the credit. When bad happens, I get the blame.

5. I make up my own mind and do what is best for me.

6. When I sin, I have to defend it—and repeat it.

7. I make a name for myself.

What God Offers

1. Peace with myself and long-range security.

2. Freedom from greed and the need for revenge.

3. The joy of helping others.

4. When good happens, I thank You. When bad happens, I ask You for help.

5. You guide my decisions, and I do what is best for me and others.

6. When I sin, I admit it. You forgive me, and You help me do better.

7. You give me Your name.

PSALM 38

Please don't be mad at me, God!
I can feel Your anger.
Every time I take a step, I'm afraid
I'll fall.
I'm afraid to answer the phone or
open a letter because it might be
bad news.

I know I was stupid.
I know I should not have done
what I did.
I try to think of ways to punish
myself.
I think that if I hurt myself
enough, I won't do such a stupid
thing again.
I hurt, I tell You; I hurt!

You know what I want, don't You?
Please hear my groans—not just
my silly words, but my screams.
My family pretends it didn't happen.
My friends won't talk to me about
it.
But they think about it and they
talk about it when I'm not there.

But I trust You, God.
I know that I can't punish myself
enough for what I did.
I know Jesus has already been
punished for me.
He could take the punishment and
survive.
I can't.

I confess my sin to You.
You have forgiven me.
Help me forgive myself.
Don't go away, God.
I need You like I've never needed
You before.

PSALM 39

I thought I had solved my problem.
"I won't talk about it," I said to
myself. "No one will know what I
have done."

I was able to avoid talking about
it, but I was not able to stop
thinking about it.
Like a commercial on TV, the
thoughts kept replaying through
my mind.

While I was having a good time
with friends, the thoughts would
attack me.
When I was trying to study, the
thoughts would take over.
In the middle of the night, the
thoughts would be there.

How can I be freed from this?
It makes my life seem like a
waste.
You're the only one I can trust,
God.
Please listen to my thoughts.
Hear them as they are.
Forgive me, Lord.
And help me find someone that I
can talk to.
Hear my prayer, Lord. Listen to
my cry.
Share my life with me, so I can be
happy.

PSALM 40

I waited for You to help me, Lord.
I waited . . . and waited.

Then You did it!

You pulled me out of my depression.

You lifted me up and gave me joy.

I am glad that I can count on You to make me happy.

I don't have to do drugs or drink alcohol to be happy.

The happiness You give doesn't make me sick the next day.

Thanks for being my friend.

Do I have to go to church today, Lord?

I know You've been good to me and all that.

I believe in You.

I pray to You.

Is that enough?

No, I don't have to go.

You won't love me any more—or less—just because I have perfect church attendance.

I don't have to go to impress You or anyone else.

But I can go to worship You because I want to.

You gave me ears to hear Your Word, and I'm going to use them.

You gave me friends who worship You, and I'm going to be with them.

You gave me friends who don't worship You, and I'm going to show them how it's done.

Lord, I know You'll always love me anyway.

That's why I want to worship You.

PSALM 41

You know I prayed for others when they were sick.

You heard my prayers, Lord, and You made those people well again.

Now I am sick.

I hurt.

For a little while, I didn't even want to live.

Those who come to see me do not help.

They say You are punishing me because I have sinned.

They say that if I really believed, You would make me well right now.

Some say I will never be well again.

But I don't care what they say.

I care what You say.

You say my sins are forgiven because Jesus is my Savior.

You say You will be with me even when I hurt and cry.

You say that I can even die, and I will live again.

That's good enough for me!

PSALM 42

Like a basketball team wants to win the play-off, I want to be with You, Lord.

I remember how I used to feel close to You.

I knew all the answers.

I sang the songs.

I said the prayers.

It seemed so easy.

But now I feel far away from You.

I ask different questions, questions with no answers.

I have new friends who have never heard of You.

I'm doing what I want to do.

Why am I so sad?

I ask You one more time:

Why have You forgotten me?

Don't You remember the fun we used to have?

Why am I so sad, and why do I have so many troubles?

Because I forgot You?

Please forget that I forgot.

I trust in You, God. You are my Savior and Friend.

PSALM 43

God, tell them You have forgiven me.

Tell them I am innocent in Your eyes.

Since You have forgiven me, why should I feel guilty because of what they say?

Send out a search party to find me Lord, and bring me back to You.

Then I will be happy again; then I will know I am with You.

Why am I so miserable?

Why do I care what others say about me?

As long as I trust in You, I know I'll be okay.

You're the only one who can save me, so keep me close to You.

PSALM 44

The Past

I've heard the story over and over again—at home, in Sunday school, in church, in confirmation class.

The story of Jesus:

His birth in a barn—Mary and Joseph, angels and shepherds.

"Oh, come, let us adore Him!"

His life on earth—He healed the sick, He told the stories, He loved the strays.

"Let us ever walk with Jesus."

His suffering and death—betrayal and denial, nails and thorns, scorn and insults.

"My God, My God, why have You abandoned Me?"

His resurrection and ascension—an empty tomb and locked room, angels and women, now He's here, now He's not. Alleluia! Alleluia!

"I know that my Redeemer lives."

The Present

Now is not like then.

You took Peter back. Why not me?

You healed the woman who touched You.

What about Grandma?

If You died for us, why did Mike die in a car wreck?

How could Lisa kill herself?

These aren't my questions, God.

Others ask me—and laugh at me.

"You go to church," they say. "Tell us about your God. Or is He too busy directing the angel choir?"

I want to hide.

I say dirty words to show that I'm not religious either, because I don't know the answers.

The Future

I still need You.

I have too many problems now.

To lose You would put me over the edge.

I will still listen to You and talk to You.

I will go to Your altar to receive You in Communion.

I will sing the songs and confess the faith.

I don't know the answers now, but I know Your love.

"Jesus loves me, this I know."

PSALM 45

At a wedding. From the left side, fifth pew: a girl's view. From the right side, sixth pew: a boy's view.

Left:

The groom looks so handsome standing there.

Is it the tux?

Or is it because he knows they are taking pictures of him?

Boys my age show off and try to act tough.

They think I should like them because they get attention.

Is he different?

Is he wonderful?

Or does he just look wonderful?

Right:

I wonder if I will ever do that.

Could I look that good?

Would a tux hide my awkward-ness?

Would it make me look sure and confident?

What girl would want me, and only me as long as she lived?

Left:

Look at her—she's beautiful!

Could I ever look like that?

Is it the dress or the hours she must have spent at the hairdresser?

She is so poised.

Would I cry or giggle if I were there?

What boy would ever want me to meet him at the altar?

Is there someone who acts silly now who will grow up to want me?

Will I be able to want one person for the rest of my life?

Right:

Wow! What a bride!

She's beautiful!

Girls I know will never look like that.

They giggle and pretend to like me; but when I try to show that I like them, they act like it's funny.

Is there a girl some place who will grow up and want me?

Center:

Some day we will walk down this aisle together.

We don't know each other now, but that's okay.

First, each of us needs to learn who we are alone before we will be able to find someone we can share life with.

God, help me be a person who loves one other person for a lifetime.

God is the one who protects us.

He is always with us, even when we are in big trouble.

We will not be afraid, even if our parents get a divorce, or if they lose their jobs, or if we have to move to another town.

Somewhere there is a place that is absolutely safe.

It is the place of God, and it is filled with joy.

God is in that place, and it will never be destroyed.

PSALM 46

God, who created us, still claims us.

Jesus, who died for us, still lives with us.

We are not afraid.

Look at what God has done for us!

Wars are fought over and over again, and yet we survive.

Violence and sickness are everywhere, and yet we survive.

Hatred rages from generation to generation, and yet His love is here.

God, who created us, still claims us.

Jesus, who died for us, still lives.

We are not afraid.

PSALM 47

Let's hear it for God!

Three cheers for God!

He is great because He has power, and He uses His power with love.

He is great because He created everything and He takes care of what He has made.

He is great because He knows how to be God.

God shows He is great by the power and wisdom of His creation and by sending His Son to be born in a barn.

God shows He is great in the splendor of nature and by giving us His Son as a sacrifice on a cross.

God shows He is great by His great throne in heaven and His Son's empty grave on earth.

Let's hear it for God!

He's the greatest!

PSALM 48

When I am in church, it seems so simple.

God is in charge of us and in love with us.

We are safe and secure. We are together.

But at school, God is a joke.

His name is used to hate instead of to love.

I have to pretend that I am cool.

I have to hide tears and hurts and fears.

I have to laugh at the new ones, the weak ones.

I have to be like those who are not like me.

But with You, God, I can be weak, and I can like those who are also weak. I can cry or laugh. I can be me.

Only then am I safe enough to love myself as I am, and others as they are.

PSALM 49

Listen up, everyone!

Pay attention!

I've got it all figured out, and I want to tell you before I lose it again.

I feel good about me. I am not afraid.

It's not because I am so good, and certainly not because I am better than others.

We can't make ourselves feel good about ourselves.

We can't put down others to lift ourselves up.

We can't make our own lives worthwhile.

But Jesus has done it for us. We don't have to deserve it. He gave Himself to be our Savior. We are worthwhile only because His death and resurrection make us worthwhile.

We don't have to make lots of money to prove how important we are.

Look what happens to rich people.

They get sick and die just like everyone else.

We don't have to become famous so everyone will know our name.

We don't have to have our pictures on TV or on the Web.

Famous people get sick and die just like everyone else.

The best way to learn how to live is to learn how to die.

Get it over with! Out of the way!

And Jesus did that for us.

He didn't just teach us how to die.

He didn't just show us the way to do it.

He did it—and He did it for us.

Now we can live without fearing death.

Those who believe in Jesus will die just like everyone else.

But we will live again with Him.

PSALM 50

Now hear this: God has something to say.

Get together and pay attention!

God says:

"You are My people because I created you, because I saved you, because I called you, because I want you to be with Me."

"I do not need you to defend Me."

"You do not make My Word true."

"You do not make My church grow."

"Your love does not save the world."

"I am not scolding you for teaching My Word, working for My church, and loving My people."

"I let you do those things because you are My people, and I want you to share My joy."

"So don't work for Me as though I need to depend on you."

"You are not doing Me a favor when you wear a cross, when you go to youth events, when you sing My praise."

"If you want to serve Me, recognize what I have done for you, and give Me the credit."

"And when you need help, ask Me for it. I will help you. Then you'll learn how to worship Me."

"Don't think that you can make up for the wrong things you do by trying to do an equal amount of good for Me."

"I have already forgiven you."

"My Son paid for your sins long ago."

"I'm glad when you believe in Him and when you love Him and want to serve Him."

"But serve Me because you are free, not because you feel guilty or because you want a favor from Me."

"Listen to what I have to say."

"Don't try to tell Me how to do My job."

"Do it with Me!"

PSALM 51

Lord, have mercy!
Because Your love has no limits!

Christ, have mercy!
Wipe away my sins!

Lord, have mercy!
And make me clean.

I'll admit that I do wrong things.

I can't forget my sins.

I have sinned against You, God,
only against You.

I have done what You told me not
to do.

You would be right if You sent me
to hell.

Sin is a part of who I am.

It has been since I became me.

Lord, have mercy!
Because Your love has no limits!

Christ, have mercy!
Wipe away my sins!

Lord, have mercy!
And make me clean.

Lord, You want me to be honest
with You.

Fill my mind with Your wisdom.

If You take away my sins, then I
will be forgiven.

If You wash me, then I will be
clean.

Lord, have mercy!
Because Your love has no limits!
Christ, have mercy!
Wipe away my sins!
Lord, have mercy!
And make me clean.

I want to laugh and sing again
I want to feel free and alive.
Erase all my sin.
Flush away all my evil.

Lord, have mercy!
Because Your love has no limits!
Christ, have mercy!
Wipe away my sins!
Lord, have mercy!
And make me clean.

Transplant a pure heart into me,
O God. You be the donor.
Give me a new and faithful atti-
tude.
Don't send me away from You.
Don't take Your Holy Spirit from
me.
Fill me with the joy of knowing
that You have saved me.
Then I will tell other sinners what
You will do for them.

Lord, have mercy!
Because Your love has no limits!
Christ, have mercy!
Wipe away my sins!
Lord, have mercy!
And make me clean.

Let me live a long life, Lord, and
let me live it for You.
Give me the ability to tell Your
Good News to others.
You don't want me to show off so
others will see how good I am.
You want me to be humble and
know that I depend on You.

Lord, have mercy!
Because Your love has no limits!
Christ, have mercy!
Wipe away my sins!
Lord, have mercy!
And make me clean.

PSALM 52

I can't understand you people!

You brag about the things you should be ashamed of.

One is proud of the fact that he has had sex with seven girls.

Another's claim to fame is the ability to drink six beers a night.

Some think they are great because they can trick their parents, others because they cheat at school.

They lie—and are proud of it!

They hate—and think it makes them important!

Don't you know you are hurting yourselves?

People may want to have sex with you, but they won't want to love you and stay with you.

Some people may think you're big stuff, but they won't trust you.

You may hold your booze now, but how long before it has a hold on you?

People who know what is right will not admire you.

They will understand that you are trying to make a name for yourself

But they depend on God.

They take the name He gave them: "Christian."

God, I am not better than others. I know that.

But I am glad that the goodness I have comes from You.

As a rose bush blooms when it is watered, I grow when You cover me with Your love.

I will always thank You, God, for what You have done.

And I want others to know that I depend on You.

PSALM 53

I caught You, God!

You gave us this one before—
Psalm 14 is the same thing.

Did You forget and repeat
Yourself?

Or are You checking us out to see
if we pay attention?

But I read it again since You said
it again.

Maybe there's a message in Your
double message.

A fool says, "There is no God."

And he says it again:
"There is no God."

And again!

And again!

The fool who says there is
no God does not make You
disappear.

My saying "There is a God" does
not make You appear.

You are what You are.

You are love—so You became
human so we could see You and
know You.

I heard Your Word that created.

I heard Your Word from a mountain.

I heard Your Word from a scroll.

And then You became the Word in
a human.

Yet sometimes we still don't hear
You, even when we see You.

So we have to be told again . . .
and again.

And the fool will still ask,
"Who's that?"

PSALM 54

Think of the power You have, God.

It can't be measured.

It can't be compared to other powers.

It can't be used up.

Use that power—all of it—to help me, Lord.

Listen to my prayer—please.

Look what others are trying to do to me.

They are trying to hurt me.

They make me feel bad about myself.

They don't care about me—or You.

But You are my helper, God.

The evil they say about me will hurt them, not me.

I am glad I can worship You, Lord.

I give You thanks because You are good.

You are with me when I need You.

You are always beside me.

PSALM 55

Listen!
Don't put me on hold!
Don't hang up on me, Lord!
I need Your help.

Bad thoughts come to my mind.
I wonder if I could die.
I wonder if I could get high and
fly away from my problems like a
bird flying toward the clouds to
escape the problems on the
ground.
I wonder if drinking beer or hard
stuff would free me from this pain.
I need some place to hide from
me.

I can take it when my enemies
hurt me.
You have answered my prayers for
help.
But now my best friend has
turned against me.
My friend, who shared my secrets,
who went to church with me!
Now my friend laughs at me
because I worship You.

I gripe and complain—and You
hear me as though You think I am
praying.
You keep promises You haven't
even made.
Yet my best friend broke the
promises that he/she made to me.

He/she talks a good line with
words that are full of pity, but
there is hatred in his/her heart.

I can trust only You, Lord, the one
friend who will not turn away from
me.
Help me be a friend to others.

PSALM 56

Have mercy on me, God.

Pay attention to me!

Look at my enemies who want to hurt me.

Look at those who mess up my life.

I am afraid, God.

I know that You, and You alone, can help me.

What can my enemies do to me if You are on my side?

My enemies have names.

Help me name them.

My enemy is Fear:

Fear that I can't be what I want to be.

Fear that I will be what I don't want to be.

Fear that I can't stay in control.

Fear that I will lose what I have.

Fear that I will kill myself, or get AIDS, or be a dope-head.

My enemy is Failure:

Have You kept a record of my failures?

Will I keep on making the same mistakes?

Am I a failure in my family?

Will I go to hell?

My enemy is The Unknown:

What will happen to me?

Will I make the same mistakes my parents make?

Will pollution or war or violence or drugs ruin the world I will live in?

I have enemies, Lord. I am paranoid.

But I also have You.

I am afraid when I am alone, but not when I know I am with You.

I can fail but not be destroyed because You are with me.

I don't have to be sure of myself because I am sure of You.

PSALM 57

Remember that You love me, God!

I see the world from two points of view.

I need Your help to know which is true.

When I sit on Your lap, I can look and see and not be afraid.

I can see my sin and not feel guilty because I know You have forgiven me.

I can see how others have hurt me and not be angry or try to get even because You have forgiven them, too.

I can see sickness, accidents, even death, and not be afraid.

I know that Jesus was a survivor—even of death—and I will be, too.

But I have another view, and it is also true.

When I jump from Your lap to the garbage pit of life, my sin becomes a big secret that hides in my gut and haunts my sleep.

Then I see the power that others have—power to hurt me, power to make me not like myself, power to make me deny You.

And I see the power I have—power to make others not like themselves, power to laugh at others, power to say and do evil.

And I see the dangers of the world—danger of ruining my whole life by one stupid choice, danger of destroying myself and my family, danger of wasting the one life I have.

Both views are true.

I need You, Lord.

Get my attention.

Dazzle me with Your glory.

Splash Your love all over the place.

Let me be so amazed by You that I never look at the other view.

PSALM 58

It's not fair, God!
It's not fair.

Parents are supposed to be fair,
aren't they?
But they're not.
And teachers aren't either.

And You're not always fair either,
God.
You've helped others when You
didn't help me.
You've given things to others that
I don't have.

What if everything were fair? We'd
all be exactly alike.
I don't know if I'd like that.
If everything were fair, we'd all be
punished for our sin.
I know I wouldn't like that.

Maybe You don't know how to be
fair, God.
But I am glad that You know how
to forgive us and how to make
each of us special in our own way.
Teach me Your way.

* See note on Psalm 35

PSALM 59

Save me from my enemies, God:
from those who drink and drive,
from those who play with guns,
from those who would give me
STDs.

I could be killed in many ways. I
know it has happened to others.

I don't have to be the one who's
dumb to be the one who dies.

Those who do stupid things take
others with them, even when they
die.

Protect me, Lord God almighty.

Don't let me think like those who
cause death.

Don't let me follow the crowd over
the edge.

Don't let me think I have to risk
my life just to show I'm cool.

Some kids want to live like they're
on a violent TV show.

But they don't have a stunt man
to take their place in a fall.

But I've got You, Lord.

You are my friend.

You love and protect me.

Teach me to follow Your way.

Why have You turned against me, God?

Don't You like me anymore?

Our team loses again and again.

My grades are going down.

My friends don't call as often as they used to.

My parents are so busy they never talk to me.

What's going on, God?

PSALM 60

And God answers:

"I have not forgotten you.

I must let you fail so you will appreciate success.

I must let you be alone so you learn to love yourself—and then you can let others love you.

I must let others be less than perfect in the way they treat you so you learn that you need to do your part in a relationship."

Okay, God, I hear You.

You haven't rejected me; You've just been loving me in strange ways.

With You as my friend, I can't lose.

PSALM 61

Listen to my problems, Lord,
problems I never thought I'd have.

For years I have wanted to be
away from home, away from family, away from classmates, away
from relatives, away from church.

And now it's happened!
I'm away.
No family!
No classmates!
No relatives!
No church!
No one!

Will You still be with me?
Can I still come to worship You?
Can I find a place to feel at home
with You when I am far from
where we used to meet?

Thanks for being with me here,
Lord.
Please stay with me wherever I
go, and I'll always look for You.

PSALM 62

Do You know how much time I
spend waiting, Lord?
I wait for the school bus.
I wait for teachers who are late for
class.
I wait for parents more than they
wait for me.
I wait in line all the time.
And I have to wait for You, too,
Lord.

Why are You so slow in answering
my prayers?
Why does it take so long to get
through to You?
I know about world population
and that other people have more
problems than I do.
But that's not supposed to make
any difference.
Do I have to take a number to talk
to You?
Couldn't You get "call waiting"?

But I have to wait on You because
I have no choice.
You don't have any competition.
There's no one else I can ask for
help.
You, and You alone, hear my
prayers.
You are the one who has saved me
from sin and death.
You know the past and hold the
future in Your hands.
I have to wait for You.
No one else will do.

PSALM 63

PSALM 64

Lord, You are on my mind all the time.

I am the sponge; You are the water.

Without You, I am dry and rough.
With You I am fresh and soft.

I like to hear Your Word and be with You in Holy Communion.

I like to thank and praise You.

You give meaning to my life.

As I go to bed, I remember You.

You have gotten me through the day.

You forgive my sin.

You help me see a happy world.

I feel You tuck me into bed like my mother used to do.

I know I have problems, and I know I make most of them for myself.

But as long as I am with You, I am safe and secure.

Hey, God, I need You!

You are my 911, my call for help.

I'm all alone.

I had friends last week; this week they are my enemies.

Last week we laughed together; this week they laugh at me.

Last week we talked together at school and on the phone; this week they talk about me.

Last week I told them my secrets; this week they tell everyone my secrets.

Come and be with me, Lord, because I am alone.

No—go be with them.

Get into their hearts and change them.

Love them so they can love me again.

PSALM 65

In the name of the Father and of the Son and of the Holy Spirit. Amen.

Here I am in church again.

I am keeping the promises that I made.

I'm here to hear Your Word, to receive You in Your Supper, to worship You and to serve You.

And You are keeping Your promises, too.

You are here with me.

You have forgiven my sins.

You are hearing my prayers.

We've got to go on meeting like this.

We have come to worship You, Almighty God, to thank You for all that You have done for us.

You have given us more than we can use and yet made us responsible for the way we use it.

You have blessed us with food, yet some are hungry because we don't share.

You have blessed us with beautiful homes, yet some are homeless unless we invite them in.

You have blessed us with beauty and resources in nature, yet we have made some things ugly and wasted others.

You have blessed us with the freedom to worship You, yet many won't unless we tell them about You.

When we say thank you among ourselves, we reply, "You're welcome."

When we say thank You to You, You say, "Share it."

I think You know us better than we know ourselves.

Jesus, You are really Great!

You're the only one who uses love
to change the world.
You're the only one who gave His
life to save all people.
You're the only one who forgives
our sins and cures our death by
giving us life again.

Jesus, You are really Great!

PSALM 66

You have helped us but do not
control us.
You have paid for us then set us
free.
You have chosen us but have not
forced us to choose You.

Jesus, You are really Great!

I will serve You because I am free
not to.
I will hear Your Word because I
want to know what You've got to
say.
I will love those whom You love,
just as You love me.

Jesus, You are really Great!

PSALM 67

God, bless our family, and keep us close to You.

Help us to share with one another the love You have given to us.

May our family praise You, O God; may all the people praise You.

God, bless all my friends, and keep us close to You.

Help us to share with one another the love You have given to us.

May all my friends praise You, O God; may all the people praise You.

God, bless our nation, and keep us close to You.

Help us to share with one another the blessings You have given to us.

May all the nations praise You, O God; may all the people praise You.

PSALM 68

God, look at Your record in history.
You always win.
Hitler thought he had You beat.
Communism thought it had replaced You.
They won some battles, but You won the war.

Some who have money and power, some who lead armies and control business think they don't need You.
Because they think they don't need You, they want You out of the way.
They fight against You.

But the poor people, the sick, the homeless, those who see their own sin instead of looking for the sin of others, the lonely, the afraid—they all need You.
Because they need You, some love You and serve You.

Look how You have led Your people.
You did not come with power to scare them or with gifts to bribe them.
But You came as one of us, a baby, in a family, in a school, in a community, in a nation.
Like us.

You gave Your perfect life for our messed up lives.
Because You died for us, we can now live for You.
People who knew You loved You so much that they told others.
Those who heard them love You so much that they told others.
(But why did some who heard the message hear it only for themselves and feel no need to tell others?)
The Good News jumped from Palestine to Africa, to Europe, to the Americas, around the world and back again.

Praise the Lord, who helps us every day.
He is the God who saves us.
He is our God, who gives us life now and forever.

(continued)

PSALM 69

We don't have to be afraid when we see His enemies win battles now.
Strong people will still depend on their own strength.
Worldly-wise people will still depend on their own wisdom.
Rich people will still depend on their money.
But we will depend on the grace of God.

Show us how You have won in the past, Lord!
Remind us that You won by dying, not by killing.
Let us see the victories You won by giving rather than by taking.

I haven't yet figured out what life means, Lord.
And I don't think many adults have either, not even those who pretend they know.
But You know about life, Lord.
You have it figured out.
So I'll just go along with You.

Prologue

Save me, Lord,

I'm in hot water up to my neck.

I'm swimming upstream.

The waves are lapping over me, and I'm about to drown.

I've called for help, but no one listens.

I have looked to You for rescue, but You are not here.

Act 1

There are a lot of people who could get me into trouble.

My sister could tell my parents.

My friend could tell the secrets that we have shared.

You, Lord, are the only one who knows everything about me.

You are the only one who knows me and loves me anyway.

I am glad I don't have any secrets from You.

I never had to worry what You would think about me if You found out because You already know.

Act 2

I cannot live in fear that others will tell on me.

I ask You to help me, God.

Help me in the time and the way that You choose.

Don't let others throw mud at me.

Don't let me be destroyed by the flood of fear that comes over me.

Act 3

You know what I want, Lord.

Get those who are out to get me!

Beat them to the punch.

Ruin their reputations before they ruin mine.

Look up their names in Your records and see their mistakes.

Tell everyone about them.

Make others laugh at them.

Act 4

But I hurt all the more when I ask You to hurt them.

Do not treat them like they treat me.

Instead, treat them like You treat me.

Let them also learn of Your love.

You listen to me when I need You; please listen to them also.

Then You can help us together.

Just as our faults have divided us, so Your love can bring us together.

*See note on Psalm 35

PSALM 70

I thought they were my friends, Lord.

They invited me to be with them.

We talked on the phone.

But now they want me to do things that would hurt me.

I know that smoking pot will hurt me.

But they want me to do it.

I know that taking drugs could kill me.

But they want me to do it.

I know that if I treated sex the way they talk about it, I would hurt myself and someone else.

Unless I do what they want me to do, I can't be their friend.

Lord, I want Your friends to be my friends, and my friends to be Your friends.

I am weak and afraid.

I need people to like me.

But I also have to like myself.

Be my friend, God.

I need You!

PSALM 71

Lord, my grandparents are old.
I didn't know that until they came
to visit this time.
I hadn't noticed that they walk
funny, that their skin is dry and
wrinkled, that they don't hear
what I say.

What will I be like when I am old?
You have always been a part of
my life.
I don't even remember a time
when I didn't know You.
Will it always be that way, Lord?
I know I will grow up. I won't
depend on my parents to support
me.
I won't always be in school, with
others teaching me.
I won't always need someone to
tell me to eat the right foods, to
go to church, to clean my room,
and brush my teeth.

But can I still be Your kid, even
when I am old?
Can I still depend on You to take
care of me?
Can I still count on You to be the
one who understands?
Yes, God! Yes!
I will always depend on You.
You will always be my God.
I will always need You.
I will cry to You for help.
And I will praise You.

Today, Lord, we studied about
government.

I learned how everything is supposed to work.

But what I learned in class is not
what I see on TV.

I learned that we are the government because we vote to elect our
leaders.

But I know lots of people who
don't vote.

I learned that we pay our taxes to
provide education, safety, justice.

But I know money is wasted and
stolen.

I learned that our leaders are public servants, selected and elected
to help all people.

But I see how they serve those
who elect them.

I see how they use their jobs for
their gain.

I see that they do not tell the
truth.

At first, I wanted to give up.

Why should I ever vote?

Why should I pay taxes?

Why should I run for office or
work for the government?

That's why I came to talk to You about it, Lord.

If I must ask the questions, I must also listen to Your answers.

You have taught me what I should be; yet I have done what I should not do and not done what I should do.

But You have not given up on me. You still love me.

You sent Jesus to be my Savior. I am forgiven.

I'm glad that I can know both what I should be and that I am loved even when I fail.

Just as I see my sin, so I can see the wrongs of my government.

It is a better government because it does not hide its wrongs—at least it doesn't always get away with things when it tries to cover up.

Our government has survived— not because it is perfect, but because it cannot always hide its imperfection.

We can survive even the bad leaders because they must face those who vote.

Lord, thank You for the government we have.

Help us to make it better.

Give Your blessings and guidance to the president and every governor, the men and women of congress, the judges and those who enforce the laws, the members of the president's cabinet, those who work in offices, those who do the little jobs.

Bless other governments, too, Lord.

Help our nation be a part of a peaceful world.

We praise You, Lord God, the Creator of all the world and all the people in it

May all the people of the world know You.

May Your name be holy everywhere.

Amen! Amen!

PSALM 73

God, I know they say You are good, and sometimes I agree.

But there are times when I can't see it.

Sometimes I think that You don't care or can't help.

It doesn't make sense to me when I see people who do bad things getting all the good things out of life.

Those who ignore You, laugh at You, and break all Your laws are strong and healthy.

They've got money.

They get good grades.

They brag about everything they do—not only the good things but also the things I'd be ashamed of.

They cheat in school, steal from stores, say awful things about parents and teachers.

And even good people listen to them and want to be their friends.

They say, "God doesn't know what we do. He's busy with the big issues of the world. He won't know what we do."

Am I stupid because I'm still a virgin, because I work for money, because I don't do drugs, because cigarette smoke makes me sick?

God, it seems to me that I get punished for doing good.

I need help from You, God.

I am talking to You because You know me better than anyone else and You love me more than anyone else.

I know that the bad things they do cause sorrow—sorrow for their parents and others now, sorrow for themselves in the future.

I know someday they will wish they had not done those things.

When I get jealous of others, I become a bitter person. I lose the joy of living.

But when I talk to You, I see things in a different way.

I am not doing You a favor when I do what You tell me to do.

You are doing me the favor when You help me do what You tell me to do.

When I do wrong, You forgive me because Jesus has been punished in my place.

But that's not all!

The same love from Jesus that forgives sin also helps me avoid sin.

I am weak, God, so weak that I must depend on You for everything.

Don't let me think that I am better than others.

Help me share Your love with others.

PSALM 74

Why don't You take better care of
Your church, God?
You gave us Your Son as our
Savior.
You called us to be Your people.
You could give us everything else,
too.
You could make us rich.
You could give us power.
You could make other people see
that You have made our hearts
different.
But You don't.

People laugh at the church and
say it is out of date.
The church never has enough
money.
The members argue with one
another.
Newscasts show church leaders
who do bad things.

They laugh at You, too, God.
They judge You by the kind of
people who claim to belong to
You.

How long are You going to put up
with it?
When will You do something?

Jesus said He came for the sinners and outcasts.
He was always looking for the lost
sheep.
I guess He got what He wanted;
He got us.
He suffered and died for people
like us.
And the church will continue to
suffer and die if it still reaches the
sinners and outcasts, if it still
goes searching for lost sheep.
Is that Your message, Lord?
Do we have to see and to show
our failures so we remember we
live on Your love?

Help us, Lord.
Help us be humble.
Help us look for mercy, not honor
and success.

PSALM 75

Thank You, God; thank You once for being You, and thank You again for the things You do.

"Some day I will come to judge you," Jesus said.
"I will be fair when I judge you, but some will be afraid.
Trust me!
Don't be scared of My judgment; I will not judge what you have done, but what I have done for you.
Think about it: You don't have to hide the bad things you've done. You don't have to brag about the good things.
I will judge you by the life I lived for you.
Trust Me on this one."

I hear You, Jesus.
If I could pick my judge, it would not be one of my teachers or a cop or one of my friends; not even my mother.
I want You to be my judge, Jesus.
I know that the ones who want to judge themselves end up proving they are guilty. The more they try to prove they are right, the more wrong they are.

But You judge me by Your grace. You give me what You want me to have instead of what I deserve.
I like that, Jesus.
I like to talk about You.
When I know You are around, life makes more sense.

PSALM 76

Everyone in town knows God; I've never seen Him in a movie or on TV. They don't give Him His own Website. He doesn't give concerts.

But everyone at school knows who He is.

They think about Him when their parents are sick, having a fight, or out of work.

They think about Him when they take a test, or when the school team almost loses.

You're so good about it, God!

You help us even when we don't ask and even though we never deserve Your help.

You seem to want to know so much about us; even when we don't want to know much about You.

Some kids say they are mad at You. You didn't do what they wanted.

They think You let bad things happen.

But I think their anger shows that at least they know who You are.

Maybe they will get mad enough to tell You—then they might even listen to You.

Then You might teach them what You taught me.

I had to learn that You're the one in charge.

I had to learn to listen to You so I could hear that You love me.

Then I could love You.

PSALM 77

Can't You hear me, God?

Do I have to turn the volume up on my prayers?

Do You know the channel I pray on?

I used to be able to sleep after I had talked to You; because I felt Your love and comfort.

But now when I think of You, I am even more worried, I am even more discouraged.

Have You forgotten all the help You gave me?

You promised to always be with me—do You still mean it?

I have enough problems of my own and I need Your help.

But now I have a greater problem: I don't think You're helping me!

I will remember what You have done.

I will see again how much Jesus loves me; I will think about His suffering—the pain He put up with for me.

I will think how He forgives sin and gives new life.

I will remember what He has done so I can see again what He is doing now.

Everything You do is perfect, God.

You know when to help us, and when to tell us to help ourselves.

You know when to hug and when to kick butt.

When Jesus lived here with us, He asked the right questions and told the right stories.

And He put His life where His mouth was when He died for us.

He even made a success out of dying by coming back to life

Man, that's good! That's real good!

You understand why I get angry at You sometimes, don't You, God?

You know I'm not good like You, and thinking about You reminds me of my faults.

Don't give up on me, God. Please!

PSALM 78

Listen, I've got something I want to teach you.

You who are my teachers, pay attention—so you will see how much I did learn.

You who haven't learned from other teachers, listen to what I have to say.

God made the whole world and everything in it.

That says it all belongs to Him, and we have to take good care of it. Okay?

And it means we all came from the same God, so we got to treat each other right. Okay?

Then God sent His Son, Jesus, to be one of us.

He did that because we messed up and did bad things.

So Jesus had to come to straighten us out.

Only He didn't do it by yelling at us or beating us.

Instead He did the good things we were supposed to do, and He gives us the credit.

Then He died as a sacrifice.

That's like He let happen to Him what should have happened to us.

Sounds bad, huh? The Good Guy dead!

But it's a good thing because He didn't stay dead. He looked Death in the face and said, "Drop dead!"

And it works: 'cause He lived, died, and lived again, we can live, die, and live again.

Now the Holy Spirit's a part of this story too.

He's the one that delivers the message.

He lets us know that God's on our side and He gives us the faith; so we can know it's true.

Now, you teachers can see that I paid a lot of attention when you taught all that stuff.

I got the message. Right!

And I'm passing it on.

Hey, you! Listen up!

Did you get what I just taught you?

PSALM 79

God, look at it!
Look at what they do to our church.
Last week someone threw a rock through a window.
Someone wrote filthy words and sprayed gang symbols on the walls of the Fellowship Hall.
I saw beer cans and condoms in the parking lot on Sunday morning.
I heard the people say: "Some kids did it!"
I wanted to scream: "An old man with a cane threw the rock. I saw a little old lady with a can of spray paint."
But it would have done no good.
Maybe it was kids that did it. It doesn't mean they think I did it.
Why do people do mean things?
Why do they destroy for no reason?
Is evil that strong in them?
Is it that strong in me—in other ways?
I wish You would punish those people, God.

But I'm glad You have forgiven me.
Thanks for being patient with me.
And just for the record: Help me be patient with those bad guys.

I know they say You are up in heaven, Lord, with all the angels, saints, and their kind.
But we need You down here, with all the users, molesters, crooks, murderers, drunks, weirdos, and their kind.
We have a problem here, Lord; this world is not a safe place to live anymore.

Bring us back to You, God! Love us and change us! Protect us from ourselves!

PSALM 80

You've got every right to be angry with us.
You tell us what to do, and we don't do it; then we blame You.

Bring us back to You, God! Love us and change us! Protect us from ourselves!

You have blessed us with many things, and we have taken credit for them.
We have used Your blessings for ourselves and not shared them with others.

Bring us back to You, God! Love us and change us! Protect us from ourselves!

PSALM 81

It's time to party! It's time to have fun!

It's the big game—the dance—VACATION!

Even the teachers seem to know we can't work today.

It's time to party!

I hear the voices plan the party:

Beer and joints.

Cars and house with parents away for the weekend.

Jokes about sex at the last party, and someone available for everyone now.

Then I hear another voice:

"I protected you at the last party. You could have been killed in the car with a drunk driver. The only reason you didn't get involved in sex was because I made you be afraid. I think it was a holy fear—good sense."

"I want you to be happy after the party. I want your happiness to last the next day. I want your happiness to make others happy too. I want you to enjoy life this weekend in a way that you can also enjoy next year."

PSALM 82

God, You are the One in charge.
You've got the power, wisdom, and love.
So tell us what You want done.
Make it clear, okay?

Okay! I've told you before and I'll tell you again:

Love Me with everything you've got.

Put Me first in your time, in your budget, and in your plans.

Read the book I gave to you.

Worship Me when you are with others and when you are alone.

Receive Jesus as He gives Himself to you in Holy Communion.

Got that one?

Okay, next:

Love other people the way you love yourself.

Talk to and about others the way you want them to talk to and about you.

If other people need your help, help them.

If you need help, ask others to give it.

When you pray for yourself, add: "And give this to others who need it too."

When you thank Me and praise Me, add: "And I thank You for blessing others too."

PSALM 83

Please, God; say something!
I'm waiting to hear You.

You've got to say something
about what is happening! Can't
You see what they write on bath-
room walls?

Don't You know they carry guns
to school?

Do You hear what they say about
You?

Are You aware of the drugs they
use even at school?

You know about the sex things
that happen around here!

Make them see what they do as
You see it.

Make them hear what they say as
You hear it.

Do something so they have to
stop long enough to hear You say:
"I am with you and love you. Your
sins are paid for and I will help
you reject the urges to do them
again."

If I can hear You, God, anyone
can.

Say it again for those who need
more volume!

PSALM 84

No one made me go to church today.

Every Sunday I complained; so they went without me.

I said I could read the Bible and pray here at home.

So I did read the Bible ('cause I knew they'd ask), and now I guess I am praying.

But it's not the same.

Everything needs a home.

A school has to have a building.

A store needs a place to sell things.

You even need a place to go if you have a job.

I can't do those things in my home. I have to go to another place.

I wonder if anyone is missing me at church today. I miss them.

I can remember to pray for them here, but will they remember to pray for me there?

When I was reading the Bible, I thought about them; they may not have thought about me.

I'm glad that You can hear my prayer now, Lord.

But next Sunday I want to be with You and others at the same time.

An hour spent with the people who love You is better than weeks spent by myself.

I would rather be in church with You and lots of people than be with You by myself.

God, You know I need to be with You.

Thanks for helping me be with others too.

PSALM 85

Thank You, God, for the things You have given to our country!

When I watch the news and pay attention in Social Science class, I get the message.

We have a great country!

It's so good that we can even gripe and complain about the things that aren't as good as we think they should be.

But some people say the whole country is going down the toilet.

Kids carry guns to school.

A lot of people can't even read a newspaper—even if they wanted to.

Half the people who get married get divorced.

Lots of babies are born to mothers who aren't married.

People cheat and lie—especially our leaders.

It doesn't sound like a good place to live.

Jesus, come to where we are and take us back to where we should be.

I hear the things You have told us: "Come, take up your cross and follow Me."

"Do to others as you would have them do to you."

"Love your neighbor as you love yourself."

"Love God with everything you've got."

It's easy for You to say those things (I know who You are), but I have a hard time doing them.

(Understand, I believe them in church; it's out here I have a problem.)

And it's hard for me to tell someone else what You said.

When I can't say it, will You help me at least show that I believe it?

PSALM 86

Let's talk this over, Jesus.
I want to hear what You have to
say about it.
I know I have no right to ask for
Your help.
I can't do anything for You to pay
You back for Your help.

But I can't get along without You.
Don't give me what I deserve.
Instead, be kind and loving to me.
Look at me after You have forgiv-
en me.

Listen to my prayer, Jesus; hear
me when I hurt inside.
I talk to You when I am in trouble
because You answer my prayers.

There is no other god like You,
Lord.
Only You have sent Your Son to
be "God with us."
Only Jesus has died to pay for
our sins.
Only Jesus has risen from the
dead with the promise that we can
die and live again.
Other gods tell us how to find
them.
You tell us how You have found
us.

Teach me about You, Lord.
Help me learn what You have done
and what I can do with You.
People try to make me forget You.
They tell me I can do it myself.
They want me to take the gifts
You have given to me and to run
away from You.

I want to stay with You.
I like me better when I am with
You.
Make my faith grow!
Help me serve You!

PSALM 87

I like to think about the place where I went to be alone when I was a little kid.

It was a place for me to hide, where I could cry, dream, pout, feel sorry for myself.

I can't go back to that place any-more—but I can be with You, Lord.

With You I can be that honest. I can even be wrong with You, because You will make me right again.

I know I'm on Your list, Jesus.

You care about me, and You check on me every day.

Don't ever forget me, Lord.

PSALM 88

GOD!
Can't You hear me?

GOD!
I've been talking to You all day.
I've said the right words: "If it be Your will, I ask this in Jesus' name."
What's going wrong?

Chris won't even talk to me anymore, and I thought we had something special.
Did we talk about things that we shouldn't have talked about?
Did we touch places that we shouldn't have touched?
I want Chris to be with me again.

My family treats me like I'm weird or something.
They don't understand when I want to be alone.
They ask me to do things that are silly and unimportant.
They think their chores are the most important things in life.

My grades are low and going lower.
My teachers are interested in what they teach—not in me.
Church is boring.
But when I don't go, I feel bad.
You're part of the problem too, Jesus.
The kids at the next table laughed at me because they saw me pray in the lunchroom.
They won't invite me to parties because I won't get drunk.

Are You going to help me now?
Or are You going to wait until I die and then take me to heaven?
Going to heaven is fine, and I'm not putting it down.
But I need Your help now—like today—as in right now.
Please talk to me! Please help me listen!

PSALM 89

God, You make my heart happy!
I want to tell everyone about You.
You love me without asking questions.
You will never give up on me.

You said, "I will send you a Savior."
And You did it!
Everyone else will tell me when I am wrong.
But Jesus is the only one who has done something about it.
He has paid for my sin.
He is with me now—and will be tomorrow.

I am happy when I am with You, Lord.
And I am happy when I am with people who are with You.
You, God, are our best friend.

Sometimes I get dizzy when I think about long ago—
before airplanes and cars,
before this country existed,
before people wore shoes,
before they knew how to make a fire,
before the world was created,
before whatever was before all of that.
I can't understand it, Lord.
But I trust that You were there before it all.

Then I look to the future and I get dizzy again.
What will happen after my parents are gone, after my house and school are gone, after I am gone?
What will be where I am now a hundred years from now?
A thousand years from now?
A million years from now?
I trust that You, Lord, will be there.

When I get confused by what is happening now, I think about things so long ago that I can't understand them; I think about things so far ahead that I can't understand them.
I can't explain the past or the future; so why should I expect to explain the present?
I am trusting You, Lord, to be here.

(continued)

It scares me when I realize that
You get angry, God.
I know what I do when I get
angry.
I know what my parents, teachers,
and friends do when they are
angry.
When people get angry, they lose
it.
They don't look or sound like
themselves.

But I'm not scared of Your anger
anymore, God.
It dawned on me that You could
just forget about me.
You don't have to stay on my case
and see me do the things that
make You angry.
If You forgot me, You wouldn't be
angry at me.

But You can't forget me because
You love me.
Jesus has promised that You will
always be with me; that means
even when I do and say things
You don't like.
Thank You for loving me, Lord,
especially when I am not lovable.

PSALM 90

Lord, You have always been the one in charge.
Before You decided to make the world, You knew that You could run it.
You've got the whole world in Your hands.

You gave me my life on Your earth.
From Your point of view I'll only be here for a moment.
To You a thousand years seems like the short break between two class periods.

I live each hour, one at a time; each day, one at a time.
Sometimes I wish days would go on fast forward so I could skip some things I don't like or get to something I want to do right now.
Sometimes I want time to stop so I can enjoy the moment over and over or so I would not have to face what is coming.
But my time is in Your hands, Lord.
If I live another day or another hundred years, You are with me and I am with You.
Thanks for Your gift of time, Lord.
Help me know I always have a future with You.

PSALM 91

What I want to say to my friend:

Look, I know you get scared—just like I do.
Let me tell you about a way out of the mess you are in.
Ask God to help you.
You may think that sounds silly, but it works.
Just say to God, "You are my God and I trust You. Be with me now and protect me."
He will hear you and stay with you.
He will go to the places you go, and He will hear the things you hear.
He will rescue you when you are in trouble—and there's more. He will help keep you out of trouble.

God will assign an angel to your case.
The angel will hang out with you and be there all the time to help you.
He will rescue you from the bad guys.

God says (look it up in Psalm 91:14-16), "Because he loves me, I will rescue him; I will protect him, for he acknowledges my name. He will call upon me, and I will answer him; I will be with him in trouble, I will deliver him and honor him. With long life I will satisfy him and show him My sal-vation."

PSALM 92

I like to thank You, God!

It makes me happy to start each day by thinking about You.

I enjoy my food, my family, my home, my school, and all the other stuff more when I remember that it all comes from You.

God, You know how to do things—and do them right!

I know a lot of people don't pay any attention to what You say.

(Sometimes I forget too.)

Some people think they can run their own lives without You.

(Once in a while I try it.)

But life makes more sense when I listen to You.

I know that what You say and do is always right.

And You are the one who takes care of me!

PSALM 93

Lord, You are at the top of the
charts!

You are the first in every league!

You take first place in all the polls!

You've got it, God!

You're the man!

Everyone else in the news comes
and goes.

My parents and teachers talk
about important people that I
never heard of.

And they don't know the ones
who are big in my life.

But You are the one who holds us
all together.

We get it right only when we follow You.

PSALM 94

Lord, a lot of people are scared of You, or angry at You, because You are the one who knows we are wrong and who punishes us.

Sometimes I feel that way too.

I don't want You to punish me.

You are too right—and I am too wrong.

Then I think:

What would the world be like if there were no one who told us when we are wrong?

No one to punish evil that hurts us and others?

We need You, Lord, to shape us up when we are wrong.

You've given us ears. Why don't we listen to You?

You've given us eyes. Why don't we see what is going on?

I know You have helped me even when I am wrong.

I know You sent Jesus to take the punishment for what I have done.

I know He forgives my sins of the past.

I know His love helps me fight temptation today.

If Jesus did not help me every day, I couldn't make it.

Lord, I am glad that You care when I do wrong.

I am glad that You correct me.

Help me also to do what is right.

PSALM 95

Praise the Lord!
> LET'S DO IT!

Sing to God with joy in our hearts!
> LET'S DO IT!

Go to God and thank Him!
> LET'S DO IT!

God is great, loving, and kind!
He is with me all the time!
God is wise, strong, and good!
I am His, He is mine!
Bow down and worship Him!
> LET'S DO IT!

Kneel before the One who made us!
> LET'S DO IT!

Lift hands to the One who saved us!
> LET'S DO IT!

Raise voices in praise to our Savior!
> LET'S DO IT!

God is great, loving, and kind!
He is with me all the time!
God is wise, strong, and good!
I am His, He is mine!

PSALM 96

Hey! It's my turn.
I get to be the lead singer!

Come on! Let's sing a new song.
No more re-runs.
No more old stories.

New Song:
Have you heard the story?
Do you know the plot?
Jesus has saved us; so thanks a lot!

Sing a new song! Tell it your way!
God is with us! I'll praise Him all day!

He died on a cross.
But could not stay dead.
He came right back.
Just like He said.

Sing a new song! Tell it your way!
God is with us! I'll praise Him all day!

I can't hold it back!
I've got to say, "Hey!
Jesus is here.
He's come to stay!"

Sing a new song! Tell it your way!
God is with us! I'll praise Him all day!

Psalm 96 is a quote from 1 Chronicles 16:23–33. The previous chapter of 1 Chronicles tells us how important it was for David to worship God. This was one of the first psalms that David asked Asaph to use to lead the people in their worship. The people liked the idea so much that they all said "Amen," and Asaph and his group (called the Levites) got the gig to be the permanent musicians for David's court.

PSALM 97

Calling Planet Earth!
Calling Planet Earth!
Good news bulletin.

God is in charge of the whole system.

You've got something more than what you stand on to hold you together.

God is God of the whole place— not just your country or your race, not just people who talk like you or believe like you.

He is the Lord of all.

God created all of us.

He shines the sun on all of us to warm us and give us light.

He lets us all enjoy the beauty of His creation and to live on the abundance He provides.

He sent His Son to pay the price of all sin and to come out of death alive so we, too, can follow Him through death and live again.

He offers all of us a new life through Baptism in His name.

He gives us Himself in bread and wine.

We get the message, God!
We know what You have done!
We know what You are doing!
Thanks a heap!

PSALM 98

Lord, I learned something new by studying something old.

I kept asking why I had to study history, all of those weird names and places and dates that I can never remember.

(I think a date should be for a boy and girl, not a war or an invention.)

But now I may have figured it out—maybe I found the answer to my own question.

Attila the Hun and Hitler both bit the dust.

The Romans and the Communists have come and gone.

The pyramids are still there, but the people and the power that made them are out of here.

Everyone who thinks they can run the world gets their day—and then they lose it.

Except for You, Lord.

You're the only One who survives.

People attack You all the time.

Some say You don't exist.

Some think they are smarter than You.

Some think they are stronger than You.

You sent Your Son to us, and we killed Him.

People always think You are out of date.

But You're always with us, Lord!

I'm glad that You'll never give up on us.

PSALM 99

Lord, I like to think about what it will be like to see You in heaven.

You must have power that makes our biggest spaceships look like firecrackers.

You must be in a place of beauty beyond the colors and shapes that we see.

You must know more than is in all of our libraries and computer files.

Yet You hang around with us.

You care when we hurt, when we are scared, and when we do wrong.

You were with Job and Jonah—Peter and the woman whose kid died.

Look, Lord, You could retire and have the good life, like Grandpa and the old guy down the street.

But You don't—and I thank You.

Thank You, God for being great and glorious and for being close and available.

Thank You, God for Your strength and wisdom and for Your love and forgiveness.

PSALM 100

I've discovered something great:
I'm happy when I worship God;
my heart is full of joy when I sing
to Him.

You want to be happy too?
Then recognize that the Lord is
your God.
He has made you; you belong to
Him.
He has connected you with other
people—we all belong to Him
together because we are His and
He is ours.

God didn't hide His love for you.
What Jesus did for you was out in
the open with lots of witnesses.
Don't hide your love for Him.
Go to church and worship with
others.
Tell Him that you know His ways
always work.
Because Jesus is our Savior, we
are connected with God and with
one another.

The Lord is good; His love has no
limits, and He will always be
faithful to us.

PSALM 101

Lord, I know the promises You have made to me.
I know You love me, forgive me, accept me.
I know You'll never leave me.

Today I make some promises to You:
I will always hear Your Word and receive You in the Supper You offer us.
I will grow in the faith You have given me.
I will not lie, cheat, and steal.
I will enjoy my sexuality as a gift from You and not use it to hurt me or others.
I will not use drugs or alcohol to escape the real world or to find short-term happiness.
I will respect my church, my family, and my nation.

I know I cannot keep these promises by myself, Lord. That's why I make them to You.
Will You help me live the way I know I should live?
Will You help me plan to do good and not allow sin to be a part of my plans?

Lord, You have already kept Your promises. Now help me keep mine too.

PSALM 102

Please listen to me, Lord.
Don't put me on hold.
I need Your help right now.
My whole life is falling apart.
My parents are angry at me.
My grades are down.
The person I like the most ignores me.
I feel guilty about what I've done.
Worse yet, I want to do it again.

I feel Your anger at me, Lord.
I even want You to be angry at me.
I want You to do something to change me.
Don't let me get away with thinking like this.
I do not want to hate myself.
I do not want to end my life.
I'm writing this down so I will remember how I feel—so maybe someday I can show it to someone else.
I need to remember that doing what I thought would be wonderful has made me miserable.
I'm just a kid, and already You have taught me how weak I am.
Is this a lesson that I will remember the rest of my life?

I know You could throw me away like junk, Lord.
But I also know that You won't.
Help me remember that You love me, so I can love myself.

PSALM 103

Let me tell you about Jesus.

Let me tell you why I love Him so much.

Let me tell you why I want you to know Him too.

He forgives all my sins—not by ignoring them or by okaying them, but by paying with His life for mine.

He makes me well when I am sick.

He not only protects me from death, but also makes me glad to be alive because He fills my life with love.

When Jesus works for the underdog, the sick, the weak, the helpless, He does not forget me.

He reminds me of the health, the strength, and the gifts I have, and invites me to be with Him and with those who need me.

I love Jesus because I can be honest with Him.

I do not have to pretend I am holy.

He takes the guilt and the memories of my sin.

He throws it so far away that I forget it.

Instead, I can remember signs of His love.

I know He is not angry with me.

I know that same love that forgave yesterday's sin will help me fight against today's temptation.

Our lives on earth are short in the mind of God, like a TV commercial that is soon over.

But our lives with Him will last forever.

Jesus has a home in heaven—and He has made a reservation there for us.

We can live here now with joy and excitement because we know our lives are in His hands.

You can live with the glory stuff—
thrones and angels, power and
might, flashing light, and things
we can't even do with special
effects.

But You don't need security
guards or fences. You don't
require appointments for us to see
You. You don't have an unlisted
number.

PSALM 104

Jesus, I like the way You operate.
You're the only one I know who's
got it all together.

With all Your big-time stuff,

You still want to hang around with
all of us. You love the people who
dress awful and smell bad.

You reach out to the drunks and
the potheads.

You are willing to be seen with the
gays and the sluts.

You even want to be with me!

You've got the power to punish,
but You forgive.

You've got the power to kill, but
You give life.

You've got the power to reject,
but You accept.

You've got me, Jesus!
And I love it!

PSALM 105

Refrain:
Jesus, come along with me.
Where I go, I want You to be.
Jesus, come along with me.
What I do, I want You to see.
Jesus, come along with me.

When I go to school and home
again,
When I play a game and do not
win,
    Refrain:

When I'm with the gang or have a
date,
Come along with me when I'm out
late.
    Refrain:

When I'm with parents and wor-
ship You,
When I'm on my own, I'll need
You too.
    Refrain:

When I look ahead, be in my plan.
Please help me to be all that I can.
    Refrain:

I don't need a judge. I see what's
wrong.
I'll need a Savior all my life long.
    Refrain:

The first part of this psalm was used by
Asaph and the Levites when they tried
out for the job as court musicians for
King David as recorded in 1 Chronicles
16. Asaph and his group sang this song
about the history of the Jewish people to
remind them that God was always with
them. Just as Asaph and the Levites only
sang a few verses for King David and
added more in Psalm 105, I have written
only a few verses of what might be part
of the story of your life. I suggest that
you add more verses as you tell about
your own life and remind yourself that
Jesus is with you.

PSALM 106

God, I thank You for being You.
You're the only one who is good,
You're the only one I can count
on.

The more I learn about what has
happened in the past, the more I
am scared about what is happening now—and what life will be like
when I am old.

I've learned about the wars—when
innocent people have been killed
by bombs, when cities were
destroyed, and people were
locked up and died.
Long ago, people in our country
even fought against one another—
and the hatred is still remembered
today.
I've found out how we have treated people of other races and
about violence and bloodshed in
our cities.
I've learned about people who
have no homes and are hungry
and that some people have not
had fair trials in court.

I see there have been bad things
even in church.
Leaders of the church argue with
one another and hurt one another.
Those who lead the church even
do bad things that cause them to
be arrested.

In my family I see people who are
angry and who drink too much.
I know about divorces, and I think
there was an abortion long ago.

I hear all the evil that others have
done, and I am scared. I am no
better than they are.
And the people around me are no
better than those who have gone
before us.

But, You, God, have always been
there.
You haven't given up on Your
people.
Please hang in with us now.
Please bless our nation, our
church, and my family.
Forgive us all for the wrong we
have done.
Help me learn from the past, and
bless me so I can do better.
I thank You, God, for being my
God.
You are the only one I can count
on.

PSALM 107

Let's sing it together because Jesus has saved us:

Sing:

God, You're so good, so very, very good.

We look at You, and we must say:

We thank You, God, in every, every way.

Some people grew up without learning about You.

They didn't know You had created them.

They didn't know You had died for them.

They didn't know they could pray to You.

But You sent someone to tell them.

You let them know that You are their friend.

Sing:

God, You're so good, so very, very good.

We look at You, and we must say:

We thank You, God, in every, every way.

Some are afraid and worry all the time.

They are afraid their parents will get divorced.

They worry about moving to another place.

They think they won't be able to graduate.

They think no one likes them.

But You let them know You are their friend.

Sing:

God, You're so good, so very, very good.

We look at You, and we must say:

We thank You, God, in every, every way.

Some worry that something is wrong with them.

They think their parents don't love them.

They think they are ugly or dumb.

They think they aren't sexy enough, or that any sexual thought makes them evil.

They think they have to brag to cover up their weak spots.

Sing:

God, You're so good, so very, very good.

We look at You, and we must say:

We thank You, God, in every, every way.

Some are afraid to show their faith in You.

They think others will laugh at them.

They think they might have to become a pastor, teacher, or missionary.

They think they might have to give their money or their time to the church.

They think they might become a religious fanatic.

But You let them know You are their Friend.

Sing:

God, You're so good, so very, very good.

We look at You, and we must say:

We thank You, God, in every, every way.

PSALM 108

Jesus, I'm counting on You.
I've got no Plan B.
You're the only Savior around, so You're the Man.

I know You love me, and I love You, but don't stop telling me.
Show Your love for me by filling my heart with good things.
Help me see Your glory in all things.

Let me hear Your words in church:
"You are forgiven because I died for you."
"Take and eat, this is My Body. Take and drink, this is My Blood."
"And I will raise you up on the last day."

I love to hear Your words of love for me.
I love to speak my words of love for You.

PSALM 109

I love You, Jesus. No problem.

It's safe to love You because You love me.

But I don't love a lot of people that You love—the ones I know You expect me to love too.

And I'm going to tell You why.

They tell lies about me—they hate me, and they want others to hate me too.

They got me in trouble in school and almost got me in trouble at home.

I tried to be friends with them, but they laughed at me and pushed me around.

So I tried to stay out of their way, but they won't let me alone.

I hope the cops get them 'cause I know some of the things they've done wrong.

Give them three months in prison, and then let them have a mean, old parole officer.

Let their parents lose their jobs, so they can't live in this neighborhood anymore.

Let them have car wrecks and have to stay in the hospital for three months.

Let them flunk out of school—and put it on their records so they can never get jobs.

LORD, GIVE MY ENEMIES WHAT THEY DESERVE!

Oops.

Treat us according to Your mercy.

*See note on Psalm 35

PSALM
110

God the Father said to Jesus, "Sit down here beside Me. You have won the battle against sin and death. You will rule with Me forever."

Jesus said to us: "Sit down here beside Me. I have won your battle against sin and death. You will live forever with Me."

As long as I can remember,
I have gone to church.
I've sat in the pew, sang the
songs, and prayed.
I've heard others stand in front
and tell me the Story.
I've listened to those in robes
and vestments.
I went up for the children's
message.
I've heard those who read the
lessons.

When will it be my turn?
When will I be the one to stand in
front of the church?
What will I have to say to the
people?

I want to say that God is real.
I know, because He answered my
prayers yesterday, and He forgave
my sins today.
I want to say that you can count
on God. He keeps His word. What
He says is true.
I want to tell everyone to pay
attention.
The way to get your life together
is to let God do the assembling.

That's what I'm going to say!

PSALM 111

PSALM 112

I've discovered something!
I've found a secret!
I'm on a roll.

This is it:

The more I worship God, the happier I am!

The happier I am, the more I worship God!

I've even figured out why it works:

When I worship God, He gets my attention.

His love makes me forget that I'm angry at others.

When He's around, I understand why He doesn't want me to sin.

His attitude rubs off on me.

I see that He protects me from misusing sex and drugs.

He gives me real joy, so I don't have to look for the fake stuff.

When I worship God, I discover that He understands me.

He's on my side and wants to help me—not by letting me get my way all the time, but by helping me love and understand others.

Now I don't have to hide from God when I sin.

Instead I talk to Him about it. He listens, and He cares!

He sees my sins as a list of problems that He has on His "to do" list, and that makes me want to worship Him even more!

PSALM 113

What will I be when I get old—30, 40, or even older?

Will I be on an Olympic team?

Will people see me on TV?

Will I be the president of our country?

Or a rich person who has planes and a house on an island all by itself?

I see the lives of the rich and famous every day.

Do they know they are on the top?

Or do they also worry about what others think about them?

Do they want to get more than they already have?

Are they afraid they'll lose their big deal in life?

Other people must look up to them, but do they know that God must stoop down to see them?

God has to bend down to see everybody.

He came down to be with us when Jesus came to be our Brother.

Jesus still comes to us, not because we can invite Him to a fancy house or send a limo to get Him.

He doesn't come because we can serve Him lobster, expensive wine, and a dessert that's on fire.

He comes to be with all of us because He loves—and likes—us.

PSALM
114

When Jesus rose from the dead,
when today we see that He is still
alive, we have a new life with Him!

He is with us—and we are with
Him!

The world celebrates His resurrection with us!

The trees get in a row and do a
line dance.

The bank buildings play leapfrog
with the government buildings!

The utility poles do a snake
dance, and the clouds play tic-tac-
toe in the sky!

Why do we see things we haven't
seen before?

Why do we let our fantasies go
wild?

How can the dull become so
exciting?

Because Jesus Christ lives!
He who has died lives again!

PSALM 115

I believe in God the Father Almighty.

You ask, "Where is God the Father? I haven't seen Him."

I answer, "When I look at the picture, I don't see a photographer, but I know one was there. When I see all the marvels of nature, I know God is there."

I believe in Jesus Christ, His only Son, our Lord.

You ask, "Where is this Jesus? Even if He was around once, where is He now?"

I answer, "Jesus is alive and well. I talked to Him this morning. I know He is here because He is God, who joined the human race. He lived like us, with a family, went to school, had a job. He was tempted like us, but unlike us He did not sin. Yet He died for our sin and rose from the dead. He lives today and will come to get us so we can live forever with Him."

I believe in God the Holy Spirit.

You ask, "Who is this Holy Spirit? Is He part of the team that includes Santa Claus, the Easter Bunny, and the Tooth Fairy?"

I answer, "The Holy Spirit brings God to me. He has connected me with all the rest who believe in Jesus. He has made me a part of the team in heaven. He gives me faith to know my sins are forgiven. He tells me I will be raised from the dead. He gives me a life that will last forever."

PSALM 116

Each time I close my eyes, I see and hear it again:

Car lights coming toward me.

The screech of brakes and the clash of metal against metal.

I see a spin, a twist, and everything upside down.

I hear screams and then a siren.

I see blood and bones, I hear my voice scream, "Please, God, save me!"

And everything goes blank.

You heard my prayer, God.

You were there in the rescue squad, in the cops and the medics, in the nurses and the doctors, in my family and friends.

I remember laying at the edge of death and knowing I was going to roll over the brink.

Then I felt You in them reach out and pull me back.

How can I thank You, Lord, for rescuing me from death?

I have said the words to You in private and in public.

I want to give to You as You have given to me.

But now, more than ever, I am aware that all that I am and all that I have is already Yours.

You have given me life.

I will live for You.

PSALM 117

Thank the Lord and sing His praise;
Tell everyone what He has done!
He sent His Son to save the world—
God's score: 10. The devil: None.

Thank You, God, because You are
good and because You are here.

It works for me.
It's a way to get the ideas in my
head and the feelings in my heart
to work together so I can say
what I think and feel.

Thank You, God, because You are
good and because You are here.

PSALM 118

When I sat in the emergency
room feeling the pain for someone
else and trying to hide my own
fear.
When I looked at doctors and
nurses and felt so grateful that
they did not drop out of school or
skip work that night.
When I saw all the equipment
they used and felt so grateful for
those who invented those things
and those who kept the machines
working,
Then I needed a way to say it:

Thank You, God, because You are
good and because You are here.

When I eat a meal and think of
those who took care of the plants
and animals, of those who planted
and harvested, those who
processed and preserved, those
who delivered and sold,
Then I need a way to say it:

Thank You, God, because You are
good and because You are here.

I look to the future and wonder
what will happen:
Will I be able to finish school?
Will jobs be available?
Will I find a good spouse (and be
a good spouse)?
Will I be able to be a parent?
Will I have good health?
Will life be worthwhile?
Then I need a way to say it:

Thank You, God, because You are
good and because You will be
there.

I listen to what people say, and
I've learned something very
strange: the name that some
people use to hate, other people
use to love.

I hear some yell "Jesus Christ!"
They mean it to hurt, to find fault,
to condemn. They use the name
to ask for evil on others.
I hear some sing "Jesus Christ!"
They mean it to love, to praise, to
forgive. They use it to ask God to
bless others.

I ask myself (and You):
By what right do I speak His
name?
Does He give me the right to
curse others for Him?
Does He give me the right to
bless others for Him?

PSALM 119

People and Places

Psalm 119, using the Hebrew alphabet (of 22 letters), was used to teach important lessons about God's Word. In the original language, each line of an eight-verse section would start with the same Hebrew letter. Following the alphabet helped the people also learn the psalm. (I'm using 22 letters from our English alphabet instead.)

The message is more important than the alphabet, so I have not changed the basic message. I am, however, personalizing it by using the names of people and places of our time to apply the message of God's will to our day.

Alyssa from Albuquerque:

I want to know the rules that God gave for me.

It makes sense to do what He has told me to do because He knows more about me than I do.

I can admit this here because no one knows my last name.

Every time I disagree with God, I discover that He is right and I am wrong.

But He loves me anyway.

Bob from Boston:

There's one good way for me to stay out of trouble—I mean trouble with parents, the cops, and at school.

That way is to listen to what God tells me and to know that He is on my side.

Chuck from Chicago:

When I try to make up my own rules for life, I feel like I'm walking with a blindfold on.

But when I listen to what God tells me, then I know the way to go.

Denise from Denver:

Sometimes I feel like giving up.

I can't do anything right.

Then I hear about Jesus and what He did for me.
He was right all the time, and I get the credit.

Evita from El Paso:

Lord, will You teach my teachers so they can teach me?
I want to know Your will and Your way.
Please help me to listen, to learn, and to do.

Felicia from Fargo:

Lord, I know You tell me what to do because You care about me and what happens to me.
I want to do what You tell me to do because I love You too.

Greg from Grand Rapids:

I always remember that You promised to help me, God, and I know You'll keep Your promise.
Now I need You to help me listen to the ways You speak to me.
I need to know You have a right to tell me how to live.

Hallie from Houston:

I know what I did was wrong and I deserve the punishment I'm getting.

I can handle it, because I know I am learning for the future, and I remember that Jesus has taken the punishment that would have condemned me to hell.

Inez from Indianapolis:

Lord, I know that doing good is more than following rules.
I used to ask You to tell me how far I could go before I crossed the line and did wrong.
Now I know that doing good is not just stopping at the line.
Rather, I do good when I go the opposite direction of sin.

Jackie from Jacksonville:

They are saying that I did bad things.
Maybe I did, but not the things that they say I did.
It hurts when they say those things, even when they're not true.
I am glad You know me, Jesus.
When You see me do something bad, You don't tell people; You forgive me.
I can live with that—and I can do better then.

(continued)

Karen from Kansas City:

God, I'm tired of confessing this same sin over and over again.

And I'm ashamed too—embarrassed that I can do better.

I know I am a sinner and that I will be until I get to heaven.

But I'd rather have a new sin each week so I would feel that, at least, I got rid of the old ones.

But here I am again, asking You to forgive the same sin by giving me Your same love and mercy.

Larry from Laramie:

It seems like the rules change every day.

My parents disagree with me and my friends.

My grandparents say my parents are wrong.

Who gets to decide what is right and what is wrong?

I'll let You decide for me, Lord,

Because You are the One who also forgives.

Marty from Milwaukee:

Lord, I love to hear Your story.

The story of how You created us.

The story of how Jesus came to be our Savior.

I like to see the pictures and hear the songs that tell me about Jesus.

When I hear Your story, I know I am a part of it.

Because I know Your story has no end, I know that my story will last forever too.

Nate from Nashville:

I like to think of my life as a long highway—with my name on it.

When I drive down my highway, I see road signs.

The signs tell me where to turn and where not.

They tell me how far I have to go and what to watch for along the way.

Your Word, God, is on all those signs.

Olivia from Omaha:

I have two ears that hear two messages.

One message is from You, Jesus.

You tell me that You love me.

You invite me to follow You and live forever.

The other message is from people who don't know You.

They tell me to forget You.

They invite me to follow them and enjoy the moment.

I have decided to listen to You.

Now I need You to help me do what You and I both want me to do.

Pete from Pittsburgh:

Don't give up on me, God!

I need to hear Your Word.

I need to know that You still care about me.

I can't make it by myself; so I will depend on You to keep my life together.

Rianna from Reno:

When I ask what is right and what is wrong, I get a lot of different answers.

My own parents don't always agree with each other, and they disagree with other parents.

My teachers have different answers to the same question.

Those who speak for the church don't always agree.

So I'll depend on You, God.

I'll read Your Word.

Even if I don't understand it all, I'll depend on You.

Sheri from St. Louis:

I know I can't always be right.

I don't have all the right answers.

I don't do all the right things.

That's why I depend on You, Jesus.

You are right for me!

You have forgiven my sins and made me right.

You know the right answers; so I'll follow You.

Tom from Tucson:

I start the day by asking: "God, will You go with me today?"

As I go to sleep I pray: "We had a good day together, Lord. Let's do it again tomorrow."

I am glad someone told me about You, Lord.

You make it all worthwhile!

Uma from Urbana:

Look at all the troubles I have!

Some of my friends are mad at me.

My parents think I have let them down.

Even Grandma sounded sad on the phone.

I realize things would be different if I had followed Your way, Lord.

(continued)

I either made or added to all the troubles I have.

Help me learn that I am better off if I follow You.

Vickie from Vicksburg:

I've figured out that life will never be easy.

Someone will always find fault with me.

I can't please everyone.

But I'm counting on You to help me, Jesus.

Others see my faults and condemn me.

You see my problems and help me.

I can't please everyone, but I want to please You.

Will from Washington:

Are You listening to me, God?

Do You know how confused and lost I am?

So many things are on my mind that I can't get through today, let alone plan for tomorrow, or next year, or a whole lifetime.

I need You, God, so I can live a day at a time and still have all my days fit together to make a long and happy life.

PSALM 120

I've learned what to do when I get in trouble:

I yell "HELP, GOD!"

Don't forget the GOD part.

Lots of people will give you help—the kind of help that gets you into more trouble.

Some people will tell you what to do, but they won't be there to rescue you when their advice doesn't work.

But God stands behind what He tells you.

You can count on Him!

PSALM 121

I look at all the people who claim to know all the answers.

I look to all of those who have the money.

I look to all of those who get to say what is right and what is wrong.

Where will my help come from?

Not from them.

My help will come from Jesus Christ, who is my Lord and Savior.

Jesus will never let you down.

He doesn't take a day off.

He won't get busy with other things and forget you.

Jesus will always love you and forgive you.

He will stand beside you now— and forever.

PSALM 122

I was glad when they asked me: "Would you like to come to church with us?"

Now we are here.

Together we confess our sins, and together we receive forgiveness from Jesus.

Together we sing our praises to Him, and together we confess our faith in Him.

Together we hear messages from the Bible, and together we hear Jesus' words: "This is My Body!" "This is My Blood!" Together we receive what He gives.

Together we give our offerings, and together we pray for one another.

I am glad that you asked me to go to church with you.

PSALM 123

Lord, I look up to see You in heaven, where You are in charge of everything.

I depend on You like a little baby depends on parents, like a house pet depends on the people who feed it.

I take a lot of abuse from others, but I can handle it; because You are in charge, and You always have mercy on me.

PSALM 124

Someone asked me "that" question.

At first I was afraid to listen to it, but I had to give an answer. "What if none of it is true? What if Jesus is not God? What if He did not live here long ago? What if someone made up the things He said and the things He did? What if He did not die to pay for our sins? Or what if He died—and stayed dead? What if He does not come back to take us to be with Him forever?"

The questions can be answered.

He did do those things long ago, and He is with us now.

If we made up the things about Jesus, we could change Him to be what we want.

But if He really did those things, then He changes us.

And I know He changes me when He loves me and forgives me.

My life is different because He is with me.

Next question?

PSALM 125

Those who trust in Jesus have got it made.

Everything else that people trust in has an expiration date.

Money can buy only so much.

Health will last only so long.

The government can do only so much.

The best school cannot teach everything.

Everybody and everything eventually have to say, "Sorry, that's all that I can do for you."

Except for Jesus!

He keeps on keeping on helping us.

He will even walk through death with us.

We can count on Him.

PSALM 126

When Jesus forgave us for the bad things we had said and we had done; when we remembered His love for each of us; when we remembered all the good times we used to have; it was like a dream!

We were happy to be together again!
We laughed together!
We told jokes.
We hugged each other.

Lord, keep us close together.
Help us understand that we always will fail; we will fail ourselves, and we will fail one another.
But You are the One who can bring us back together.
You are the One who can keep us together.

PSALM
127

Sometimes I get scared when I think of the future.

I see so many people who have messed up their lives.

They're hooked on drugs; or they're angry at everyone; or they have to show off all the time; or they act like they don't care about anyone.

Then I remember You, Lord.

I include You in my plans for the future.

Unless I look forward to a life with You, I'll be like those who already have run into a brick wall.

Then I remember my parents.

Even though they don't always understand and they think I have to live the way they do, I know they are a gift from You.

At least they would help me if the advice they gave me goes wrong.

Help me listen to You and others who help me plan for the future.

PSALM 128

Lord, I've found the way to get along with people.

It's so simple!

First I must get along with You.

I've got to be honest with You, admit my mistakes, accept Your forgiveness, and talk to You even when I'm not in deep trouble.

When I feel good about You, I can feel good about myself.

I don't expect to be perfect— You've done that for me.

I don't have to give up—You help me accept things as they are.

Then I can face the world! School's okay 'cause I'm in there trying.

I can live with my family 'cause they're okay too.

Other people still cause problems for me, but I know I can't change them.

But You change me; so it all works out.

Thanks, Jesus! I don't know what I'd do without You.

PSALM 129

God asks:

Tell Me, young person, how many ways have you already been hurt in life?

Check the list to see where your pains are:

I have been called stupid and dumb.

I have been physically abused.

I have been teased by other kids.

I have been sexually molested.

I have been accused of things I didn't do.

I have been told I don't do anything right.

I have been told I'm fat, or skinny, or ugly.

I have been made to think that all my private parts are too small.

I have been told that I am clumsy.

I have been told my family is no good.

_____
(add your own)

I have looked at your list.

Now look at the list that I have made for you:

I love you the way I have created you.

I accept you the way you are.

I forgive all that you have done wrong.

I will help you be all that you can be.

I will always be your Friend.

PSALM 130

Lord, I'm at the edge!
I see no way out.
I thought about killing myself;
then I remembered You.
Please listen to me!
You're the only One who can
help me.
I know You have forgiven me.
I know You don't even keep a
record of the wrongs that I have
done.

Now I wait for You to help
me again.
Just as I wait for the last school
bell on Friday afternoon, so I wait
for You to answer my prayer.

I trust You, Lord Jesus.
I trust You to save me, because I
cannot save myself.

PSALM 132

PSALM 131

Jesus, You have helped me.

Because of You I don't have to be right all the time.

I don't have to pretend I know all the answers.

I don't have to win every game.

Now I feel good about myself.

I am at peace—like when I was a little kid sitting on my mother's lap.

God, don't forget who Jesus is!

I know He's Your Son—and I like all that glory stuff.

But He's also my Brother.

He learned how to hurt and to cry.

He knows what it's like to be frustrated and disappointed.

He was even tempted to sin—in every way that I have been.

That scares me 'cause I've got some temptations I can't talk about.

But He knows about them.

Don't forget that, please!

I read the promises Jesus made to us.

Keep those promises too! Please.

PSALM 133

I like it when everyone at home likes each other—when we laugh and tell jokes; when we hug each other; when we listen to each other; even when we cry together because we care.

I like it when home is the place I want to be.

PSALM 134

Lord, bless me as I go to sleep.

Also bless those who must stay awake to protect me during the night and to provide what I need tomorrow.

In Jesus' name. Amen.

PSALM 135

God I checked out Your competition—the other gods that I see my friends serving.

Some worship sex.

One guy I know even has a little statue of sexual organs.

Some worship money.

They make it their goal in life.

Some worship a good time.

They'll risk all of their future for one moment of fun.

I worship You, Lord.

Other gods make us think of ourselves and what we get, but You love us in a way that lets us love others.

You created me—

and that means You created everyone else too.

Jesus is my Savior—

and that means He died and lives for everyone else too.

You want me to be with You—

and that means You want the rest too.

Lord, You're the only One who makes Yourself, them, and me into US.

I like me better when You and I are We.

I like others better when they and I are We.

PSALM 136

God is great! God is real!
Thank You, God, for this meal!

God is great! God is cool!
Thank You, God, for our school!

God is great! God is wise!
Thank You, God, for our lives!

God is great! God is true!
Thank You, God, for being You!

God is great! God is near!
Thank You, God, for being here!

God is great! God has power!
Thank You, God, for each hour!

God is great! God is fun!
Thank You, God, for what You've
done!

PSALM 137

Here I am in a strange house in a strange town.

I go to a school and a church where nobody knows my name.

My parents tell me that this is now our home—that I must look to the future and make friends here and not think of my old friends where we used to live.

That may be good advice.

I agree that it makes sense.

But it doesn't work.

New friends don't replace old friends.

Part of who I am came from where I used to live.

Now I've got to learn to be me again.

At least You, Lord, have moved with me.

I need You now more than ever.

PSALM 138

How can I thank You, God?
Let me count the ways:

I can tell You how much I appreciate You as I am doing right now.

I can thank You by joining with others to sing and to say our words of gratitude as we do every Sunday.

I can kneel before You and hear that You gave thanks when You gave the bread and wine with Your words, "This is My body; This is My blood." And I can give thanks that I can receive what You have given.

I can use Your name and mean it.

I can give You gifts of thanksgiving by giving to those whom You also love.

If You can think of some more ways, let me know. I'm listening.

PSALM 139

Lord, You know everything about me—more than I know about myself.

I don't want many people to see me naked, but You see more than how I look without clothes or decorations.

You see inside of me and know all that I think, all that I feel, all that I am.

And yet You love me.

I'm glad that You already know everything about me.

I don't worry that sometime You will find out something I said or did and not love me anymore.

Before I was born, You planned for me.

You put me together through the love of my parents.

Before they knew about me, You already loved me.

Keep on checking me out, Lord.

Find every evil in me and forgive me.

Find every good in me and give me ways to use it.

PSALM 140

Lord, I don't even like myself anymore because no one else does.

Other kids at school laugh at me.
They say I'm a nerd and that I
dress weird.

My parents tell me that I'll never
amount to anything.

My brother said he didn't want
anyone to know that we are
related.

I can't defend myself, because I
am not a credible witness.

But You are my God, You are my
Savior.

I've read Your Book, and I know
You stick up for losers.

By myself, I am a loser.

Please don't ever let me be by
myself.

Please protect me and keep me
with You.

PSALM 141

Lord, as I look back on today, I realize how much trouble I made for myself.

Please put my mouth on restriction.

Tell me to shut up.

You don't even have to be polite about it.

I know I went around bragging all day.

I tried to make myself sound cool.

I was loud. I said dumb things about other people.

I blamed others for what I had done. I even misused Your name to make me sound tough.

I have to face those people tomorrow.

That's why I want to talk to You tonight.

I can admit my mistakes to You 'cause I know You'll forgive me.

But if I admit to them I was stupid, they'll laugh at me and put me down.

I think I've made a mess of things.

Will You show me a way out?

PSALM 142

God, as I pray to You, I pretend I hear an angel's voice: "Your prayer is being received. If you have a request, press 1. If you want to give thanks, press 2. If you want to praise God, press 3. If you have a complaint, press 4."

I'm pressing 4, God.
I've got a complaint, and You're the only one who will listen.

I'm in trouble for everything I do. I know I shouldn't drink beer, but everyone else does. I have thoughts about sex that scare me; I don't want anyone to know about them. I don't care about what happens at school and at home.

Please help me, Jesus!
Please listen to my complaints.
Give me Your love and acceptance; then I can press 2 and 3.

PSALM 143

Please listen, God!

Put on Your glasses—the ones with the cross etched in the lens— and see me as one forgiven by Jesus.

Don't blame me for all the things I've said and done.

Forget the things You heard me think.

I remember how I've felt shame before, and You have comforted me.

I promised that I'd do better—and I thought I would—but here I am again asking for Your mercy.

Save me, God!

Not only from the enemies around me, but also from the enemies inside me.

PSALM 144

Lord, I know that I am one of billions of people.

I can't figure out how You keep track of each of us. But that's okay. It's Your job—I won't mess with it.

My job is to know about You, and I need help!

Poke Your finger through the sky and zip it open from east to west; then pry the sides apart.

Peak down through the opening and say, "Hi!"

Then we'll all know that You're up there, and we'll know that You care about us down here.

Even as I ask You to show Yourself, I remember that You've already done it.

The shepherds saw angels in the sky and went to the manger to see Your Son.

Because He died for me and rose again, I know He still loves me.

That means He is still with me, and with Him I'll make it.

PSALM 145

I want to get You on TV, Jesus—
Your own program!

A full hour—with no commercials!

And I want to be the emcee who
introduces You.

I'll tell everyone what You have
done for me.

I'll say You're the only one who
has beat the hell out of sin and
death.

Then I want You to talk.

Don't forget those good lines You
have:

"I will be with you always!"

"Follow Me!"

"Whichever one of you is without
sin may throw the first stone."

"Do not be worried and upset."

"I am the Way, the Truth, and the
Life; no one goes to the Father
but by Me."

"This is My body; this is My
blood!"

I just love the way You talk.

PSALM 146

Jesus, will You help me find something good in what happened—and didn't happen—today?

I felt alone all day.

Everyone in my family was so worried and busy that none of them had time for me.

My friends all were wrapped up in their own problems.

My teachers didn't seem to like school any more than I did.

I called Jim and left a message on his machine, but he hasn't returned the call.

You're the only one who has time for me, Lord.

Maybe that's what I learned today.

I know the others do care about me, but they are like me: they have problems too.

Don't You have any problems, Lord?

How can You spend all Your time loving us and not take time out for Yourself?

I thank You, Lord, for being with me, for hearing my prayers, and giving me a new start for tomorrow.

PSALM 147

Jesus, I've figured it out.

You're the one in charge.

You've made the plans for all of us—and for each of us.

You followed the plan Your Father gave You when You came to live with us, when You died for us, and when You came back to life again.

You didn't just tell us what to do or show us what to do, You did it for us.

I still can't follow Your plan exactly, but You put me back on track each morning and You go with me each day.

Thank You, Jesus.

PSALM 148

Let's have a parade!

Let everyone who wants to praise God get in line.

Angels, warm up your voices and take the first place.

Sun, slip out of orbit and lead the moon and stars down our street.

Mountains and trees, put on wheels and roll into place.

Animals and birds, people of fame and power, people unknown and weak, dance together as we

PRAISE THE LORD!

PSALM 149

There are some things I can do alone, but they are more fun when I share with others: eating, listening to music, cheering the winning team, worshiping God.

With my friends, family, and strangers, I sing praises to God our Savior.
With a congregation, I hear that God loves us, and together we show our love to Him.

I thank You for blessing me, Lord.
Thank You for blessing others in the same way, so we can come together to praise You.

PSALM 150

I'm invited to a party—a party to praise God!

What will I need to take along?
I will praise Him with the CD I love to hear.
I will praise Him with the video game I love to play.
I will praise Him with the food I eat.
I will praise Him with the clothes I wear.
I will praise Him with the words I speak.
I will praise Him with the friends I hang out with.
I will praise Him with all that I am, all that I do, and all that I have.

PRAISE THE LORD!

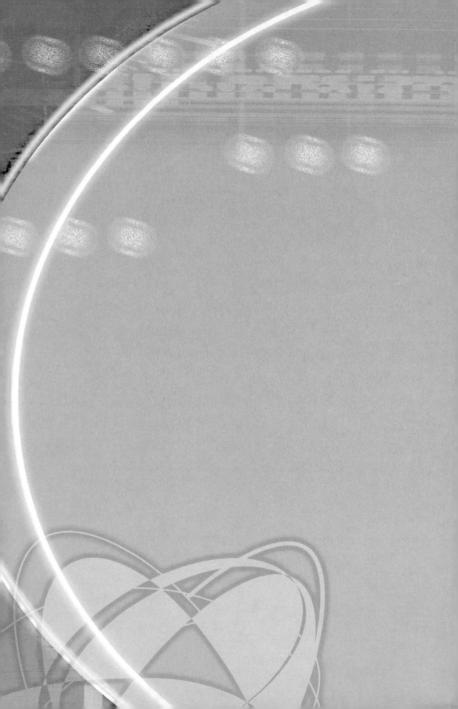